The
CHOSEN

BOOK TWO

40 DAYS WITH JESUS

By
Amanda Jenkins,
Kristen Hendricks,
& Dallas Jenkins

BroadStreet
PUBLISHING

CONTENTS

FOREWORD

I remember the first time I watched *The Chosen* series. I had heard about it from some of the crewmembers who had worked on the set. Many of them had helped me produce our own films, so I knew that their endorsement of this biblical series deserved my attention. I'll admit that when I finished viewing it, I rewatched the whole thing again with my family. Not only was it well made, but it also ministered to me. I found myself wondering what I would have acted like had I been there with Jesus. Would I have freely given my opinion like Peter? Would I have tried to calculate His actions like Matthew? Or would I have followed Him in awe like Mary, clinging to His every word?

I imagined walking with Him daily, watching His kindness, His patience, and the way He displayed His love to others. Yes, I would have felt thrilled to see a miracle up close, but to sit and eat with Him the way His followers did or to have a one-on-one conversation with Him to share my questions, thoughts, and concerns…well that would have been unbelievably amazing!

And yet, we can *still* do that.

The fact that this same Jesus who walked the earth with the disciples is *still* alive today and wants to spend personal time daily with each of us is *still* amazing! He sent His own spirit to dwell in us, to guide us, and to help us. He *still* longs to hear our questions, thoughts, and concerns. He *still* wants to love others through us. He *still* wants to do miracles! And He *still* says to us, "Follow me."

As you read these devotionals, don't forget that the One who loves you so much that He gave His own life wants a growing relationship with *you*. He wants to walk with you, to love you, and to show you more of who He is. And He patiently waits for you to respond to His invitation.

So find that quiet place each day where you and Jesus can meet. Worship Him from your heart. Thank Him for all He's done. Listen for Him to speak in that gentle, quiet voice as you read His Word. And take comfort in the fact that He *still* sees you, loves you, and has chosen you.

Alex Kendrick

Writer, Director

NEW BOOK,
NEW QUESTION

For our first book, the questions governing each devotional were:

1. What don't we know about these people?

2. What should we know about these people?

3. How will going from not knowing about these people to knowing about these people change us and other people?

Answers: Plenty. Everything. A lot.

As the stories of Mary, Peter, Nicodemus, and Matthew unspooled and intertwined, we came to appreciate this obvious truth in a whole new way: every detail matters. Every exchange is deserving of thorough examination and deep contemplation, as well as the setting and context in which they reside. Without exception, every aspect of their no-picnic lives offers us another breadcrumb along the trail.

Out of the four, Nicodemus was who we knew the least. Studying him was like finally connecting with a complicated uncle. We feel like we get the guy now and look forward to seeing him at family gatherings. Matthew and Peter are our brothers now. And Mary! Mary's our girl. We're very close.

As serendipitous as knowing about and relating to certain Bible characters can be, it doesn't hold a candle to understanding the lengths to which Jesus will go to relate to us so we can know Him. That's the purpose of every person's story in the Bible: to aid in the supernatural revelation of Jesus Christ.

In other words:

– Because we know Nicodemus better, we now know Jesus better.

– Because we know Matthew better, we now know Jesus better.

– Because we know Peter better, we now know Jesus better.

– Because we know Mary better, we now know Jesus better.

That's it. That's what makes these folks so wonderful. Through their stories we're able to see Jesus' compassion, patience, mercy, love, and redemption. Because of these guys (and so many others), we can start to wrap our brains and hearts around how Jesus feels toward us. And, of course, it's a tremendous help knowing they were all such a mess—through them we can see more clearly the only Way to be whole.

So now, with this second devotional book, we're switching gears a bit. Instead of three overarching questions about the people around Jesus, this new batch is predicated on one penetrating question: *What does it mean to reeeeeally follow Jesus?*

Not just showing up periodically, hoping to get a meal or a healing, but going all in and following Him wherever He may lead…like, say, to a cross.

We hope you, too, will appreciate and contemplate the details in a whole new way, as we have. And we humbly pray this devotional will aid in your supernatural revelation of Jesus Christ, as it has for us.

Amanda, Kristen, and Dallas

IDENTITY

When Jesus came into the district of Caesarea Philippi, he asked his disciples, "Who do people say that the Son of Man is?" And they said, "Some say John the Baptist, others say Elijah, and others Jeremiah or one of the prophets." He said to them, "But who do you say that I am?" Simon Peter replied, "You are the Christ, the Son of the living God." And Jesus answered him, "Blessed are you, Simon Bar-Jonah! For flesh and blood has not revealed this to you, but my Father who is in heaven. And I tell you, you are Peter, and on this rock I will build my church, and the gates of hell shall not prevail against it."

MATTHEW 16:13–18

Not every miracle was jaw-droppingly epic. There were levels. One miracle was so low-key it would've gone undetected had Jesus not pointed it out. It happened during a private conversation between Jesus and the disciples.

He asked them who they thought He was.

Simon Peter answered that He was the Christ, the Son of the living God.

Boom. Miracle.

Compared to watching Jesus multiply fish, heal lepers, and exorcise demons, this miracle might've lacked some of the wow factor they'd grown accustomed to. Nevertheless, what transpired during that short conversation was profoundly more life changing. It wasn't Jesus demonstrating His authority to the masses. It was the Father revealing His Son's identity to the individual.

Jesus hadn't yet explicitly taught them the fullness of His identity. Hence, Peter's answer was not a foregone conclusion. Nor was it a go-big-or-go-home guess. It was a supernatural revelation imparted by the Maker of the universe—a miracle so personal and powerful that nothing in Peter's life would ever be the same.

Conversely, let's look at the other folks' answers. John the Baptist was a decent guess since He, too, was a homeless, radical preacher. Elijah performed some pretty mind-blowing miracles. And, like Jesus, Jeremiah preached boldly and prophesied in the temple courts. These weren't the worst theories ever, but the supernatural revelation part was clearly lacking.

The people assumed that Jesus was a second act rendition of a former spiritual heavyweight. They couldn't conceive of Him being wholly original. But that's what people who don't know Jesus tend to do—they cobble together a sort-of plausible, albeit totally wrong, assumption regarding who or what He's like.

And the only remedy to our half-baked human explanations is supernatural revelation from God. He has to open our eyes.

And once He opens our eyes? It is only then we understand just how unrivaled He truly is. Simon Peter was the first disciple to see it; the Father revealed to Peter who Jesus was: The Christ. And then Jesus revealed to Simon Peter who Peter was: The Rock on which the church would be built. One identity affirmed the other.

He's eager to do the same for us. *Who do* you *say I am* is a question Jesus asks every single person. Once we can see that He is the Christ and we surrender our lives to Him, He affirms our identity: We are chosen. We have been redeemed. We have been summoned by name, and we are His. This miracle is so personal and so powerful that nothing in our lives will ever be the same. Low-key as the act may seem to be on the surface, there is nothing more jaw-droppingly epic than knowing Jesus Christ, the Son of the living God.

PRAYER FOCUS

Praise God that He is eager to reveal His Son to those who are seeking. Ask the Father to open your eyes to His identity if you don't yet know Him. Ask for a greater comprehension of it if you do. Thank Him for choosing you and for such a personal and powerful miracle.

MOVING FORWARD

o   Who do you say Jesus is?

o   If you know Jesus, describe the moment His identity was revealed to you and how you responded. If you don't know Jesus yet, describe what you've assumed or understood about Him thus far.

o   How does Christ's true identity impact, clarify, and solidify your own identity?

AMONG US

There is in Jerusalem by the Sheep Gate a pool, in Aramaic
called Bethesda, which has five roofed colonnades.
In these lay a multitude of invalids—blind, lame, and
paralyzed. One man was there who had been an invalid
for thirty-eight years. When Jesus saw him lying there
and knew that he had already been there a long time, he
said to him, "Do you want to be healed?" The sick man
answered him, "Sir, I have no one to put me into the pool
when the water is stirred up, and while I am going another
steps down before me." Jesus said to him, "Get up, take up
your bed, and walk." And at once the man was healed, and
he took up his bed and walked.

JOHN 5:2–9

The Sunday school reaction to this miraculous story
is to think it's awesome and wonderful and happy—the
flannelgraph scene would, no doubt, be all smiles. But

15

perhaps a more appropriate response is heartbreak because thirty-eight years is a soul-crushing length of time. And this man's soul had been crushed.

The scene was brutal. A sea of sick and disabled people were all lying beside the pool of Bethesda, hoping to be healed in the water the way others were rumored to have been. Unpredictably, the underground spring that fed the forty-five-foot-deep pool would cause the water to well up. Bubbles would rise along with sediment from the basin floor—no doubt the minerals in the sediment, along with the fresh water, delivered health benefits. But over time, the people attributed the natural spring and its side effects to spirits, so when the water moved, the people rushed in hoping for a miracle.

But not everyone. Not the man who was so sick for so long that he'd given up even trying. He had no ability to help himself, no way to reach the water, and no one in his life who cared enough to get him there.

Enter Jesus.

What was it like for the Creator, Redeemer, and Healer to walk among the suffering? Certainly His heart broke, and not only because of the people's pain, but also because of their misplaced hope. Or total lack of hope.

"Do you want to be healed?"

What a strange question because of course the guy did. Every person with a physical affliction in that place wanted to be healed; it's why they were there. But no one seemed to take notice of the One who was actually able to heal them. Jesus walked among them—the sick and diseased, the deaf, blind and lame—while they focused their time and energy and hope on the water. Which is what we all do to some degree. We focus on our struggles and the solutions we work out in our heads while our Creator, Redeemer, and Healer is among us.

"Do you want to be healed?"

The man answered Him, "Sir, I have no one to put me in the pool when the water is stirred up, and while I am going, another steps down before me." In other words—*of course I want to be healed, are you nuts? But I gave up trying a long time ago because it's impossible. I'm totally alone, and I'm going to live out the rest of my pathetic days on this mat.*

It didn't upset Jesus that the sick man didn't immediately understand His offer. We oftentimes don't. Our human tendency is to underestimate Jesus—or to not estimate Him at all. We get so stuck in our circumstances and in how we see the world that we don't notice or comprehend what's being offered.

We don't see that our rescuer is stooping low, and no doubt that's exactly what Jesus was doing—kneeling at eye-level when He spoke to the man with no hope. No doubt the sound of His voice was kind. No doubt His demeanor was patient. Quiet. No doubt there was overwhelming compassion in His eyes as He extended Himself to the one who had no idea his rescue was imminent.

"Do you want to be healed?"

The only thing more heartbreaking than being sick and alone for thirty-eight years would've been for this man to walk home and forget the One who healed him. What a waste if his physical transformation didn't result in a spiritual one. Because that's the transformation that matters most and is offered to all—the spiritual. How tragic that so many people forgo soul healing and on-going relationship with Jesus. And how unnecessary that even after we know the Savior, we continue to cling to the sick and diseased parts of our hearts instead of looking to Him for healing again and again.

Do you want to be healed?

Because He's still among us.

PRAYER FOCUS

Meditate on Jesus. Thank Him for being so near. Ask Him to show you how to get your eyes off your own solutions and to look to Him for help and hope.

MOVING FORWARD

o   What circumstances are you managing in your own strength, power, or wisdom?

o   Read Jeremiah 17:14. Be specific with the Lord about what you think you need help with and healing from. Then ask Him to show you what *He* thinks because so often our thoughts are not His thoughts (Isaiah 55:8–9). While God doesn't say *yes* to healing every physical ailment, He promises us His presence and strength and the hope of a pain-free eternity. Talk to Him about what ails you and trust Him with it.

o   Once Jesus healed the sick man at Bethesda, He told him to "get up, take up [his] mat, and walk." In what ways do you need to get up? Because once we're healed, physically or spiritually, it's time to act like it.

LONELY PLACE

Jesus often withdrew to lonely places and prayed.

LUKE 5:16 NIV

In Psalm 25, David's emotional distress has reached a fever pitch. He's lonely. He's afflicted. He's troubled. He's altogether beside himself. So in true David fashion, he cries out to the Lord pleading for rescue. "Turn to me and be gracious to me, for I am lonely and afflicted. The troubles of my heart are enlarged; bring me out of my distresses" (Psalm 25:16–17).

In the New Testament, not one person is described as lonely. Obviously, there were still plenty of lonely people. Take the Samaritan woman for example. Her troubled life left her void of true companionship. She was emotionally distressed. It was probably the reason she was at the well in the first place.

In the Gospels, lonely isn't a condition; it's a *place*. It's where Jesus withdrew to spend time with His Father. He did this often and would occasionally stay and pray throughout the night. What did He pray? We don't know, exactly—at least not to the extent that we know David's prayers.

Jesus' lonely place was the stuff of intrigue. The disciples recognized that something much deeper was happening there—something worth forfeiting entire nights of sleep. Once, after Jesus returned from the lonely place, the disciples asked Him if He'd teach them to pray; they wanted to understand. Jesus broke it down by way of the Lord's Prayer: Honor God. Seek His perfect will. Ask for what you need. Expect it. Forgive. Honor God.

That's the formula David had down pat. In his loneliness he sought the Lord. He asked for relief and expected it. He repeatedly petitioned God to show him what to do and to guide his every step. David knew full well that he could not do life on his own. And so did Jesus.

In fact, Jesus stated numerous times that He could do nothing by His own authority. He was completely dependent on and obedient to the Father. Perhaps it was in the lonely place where He received the bulk of His instruction. Perhaps many of His prayers were similar to those of David's. No doubt, it was in the lonely place where Jesus could find rest and be fully known, even the night He sweat drops of blood while pleading for God to spare Him from His impending suffering.

And God chose to rescue us instead.

It's befitting that no one in the New Testament is described as lonely. The presence of Jesus eradicates it. Emotional distress has been transformed into the meeting place where Jesus turns to us and is gracious to us. Take the Samaritan woman for example. It was in the lonely place where Jesus met her, relieved the troubles of her heart, and freed her from her anguish. With Him, she discovered we are never void of true companionship. With Him, we find our rest and are fully known. With Him, we are never alone.

PRAYER FOCUS

Praise the Lord that He transforms the condition of loneliness into a meeting place with Him. Ask Him for comfort, direction, rest, and freedom from any distress. Ask God to make Himself known to you and expect it. Thank Him for being a true companion and for never leaving or forsaking you.

MOVING FORWARD

o   In what ways has loneliness affected your life?

o   What is your default response to loneliness? Do you cry out to the Lord pleading for rescue? Or like the Samaritan woman did before she met Jesus, do you take matters into your own hands and avoid painful situations?

o   How has Jesus turned to you and been gracious to you in your loneliness?

ENDGAME

[Jesus] went throughout all Galilee, teaching in their synagogues and proclaiming the gospel of the kingdom, and healing every disease and every affliction among the people. So his fame spread throughout all of Syria, and they brought him all the sick, those afflicted with various diseases and pains, those oppressed by demons, those having seizures, and paralytics, and he healed them.

MATTHEW 4:23–24

Jesus was leading a growing caravan—because of course He was. According to Matthew, no one was turned away; all who came to Jesus for healing were healed (it's a wonder the crowds *ever* dissipated). So yeah, it would've been something to see, and by all accounts it was an extremely successful public ministry launch, since word of the carpenter's-son-turned-miracle-worker spread like wild fire—because of course it did.

But it wasn't just a healing tent party. Jesus was *proclaiming the gospel of the kingdom,* which is an easy part of these verses to overlook since it's healing that fills the proverbial seats, and by comparison, preaching is so much less interesting. But Jesus' message of salvation was the whole point, which means the miracles were a way to draw people in and convince them to stay, listen, and hopefully believe the guy in the pulpit.

The miracles confirmed the message.

That said, suffering does have a way of making itself the main thing. Not only is it really hard to cope with physical and emotional pain on a daily basis, it's also difficult to reconcile suffering's very existence with a loving God. In other words, if God is loving, why does He allow suffering in the first place? And because that's a totally legitimate question, some people don't even stick around for an answer. For so many, the question itself becomes a resolved statement of disbelief—of rejection. People reject God based on the fact that He allows suffering.

Conversely, people ran en masse to the God-man based solely on the fact that He was ending their suffering—*which means their pain drove them to Jesus.* And now we're getting somewhere because, unfortunately, pain—or rather, needing relief from pain—is often the reason some of us seek God or cling to Him. It's simply not our human tendency to surrender our hearts when everything is fine. We don't often seek help in abundance or change course when the road is smooth. Sadly, we all need a healthy dose of desperation to recognize our need and our total inability to meet our need.

So if suffering causes otherwise independent, self-sufficient people to run to Jesus, and believing Jesus' message is the key to spending eternity with Him in heaven, then doesn't it stand to reason that there's eternal purpose in suffering? Without it, the crowds would not have flocked to Jesus, and they would not have heard His message of salvation and life-everlasting. Moreover, without pain and desperation, our hearts tend to wander away from Jesus even after we've embraced Him as Savior. Comfort brings ease; with ease, we cease to seek, so pain tends to be a spiritual blessing in disguise our whole lives long.

Like healing, suffering is not the end—it serves the endgame. That's not to say that suffering isn't heartbreaking; it broke Jesus' heart. Over and over, the Bible says He had compassion for people who were suffering. But He also understood its purpose because He sees beyond temporal, earthly moments to eternity, and He's willing to endure pain—even His own unspeakable suffering on the cross—to ensure we have every opportunity to spend a pain-free eternity with Him in heaven.

Because of course He is.

PRAYER FOCUS

God knows your pain, and He has tremendous compassion for you. Pour your heart out to Him—tell Him about your suffering. But also ask for help to trust Him more, knowing the things He allows have an eternal purpose. Rest in knowing that healing will come, on earth or in heaven.

MOVING FORWARD

o In your own words, explain why a loving God allows pain.

o Job suffered. John the Baptist suffered. Paul suffered. The list goes on. But all three men were monumentally used by God to build His kingdom and point people to Jesus. What does their suffering teach you about your own?

o Read Revelation 21:3–4. Healing is a certainty for all who believe because God promises heaven will be pain-free. How does knowing what lies ahead impact what you're dealing with today?

DAY 5

DESPERATE

Jesus said to him, "Go; your son will live."
The man believed the word that Jesus spoke to him
and went on his way.

JOHN 4:50

Desperation makes us do unconventional things. It prompts us to seek answers in places we wouldn't normally go and elicit help from people we wouldn't normally talk to. It chucks pretense out the window. It makes us vulnerable. Desperation forces us to see life through a different lens and is often the very thing that drives us to Jesus.

In John chapter 4, there's a royal official who's all too familiar with that kind of reckless desperation. His son is sick. Dying. The second he hears that Jesus is back in Cana, he takes off from Capernaum, which was a twenty-mile hike. That's a lot of time to think and worry and fear the worst. When he finally gets to Jesus, he begs Him to heal his son.

I (Kristen) understand this parent because I was this

parent. Pleading for the healing of my daughter is the very thing that drove me to Jesus. Like the royal official, I didn't actually know Him, but I'd heard about what He could do. I grew up in church, learned the age-appropriate versions of Bible stories, and glued and glittered the corresponding crafts. I was always aware that Jesus performed miracles; I just never cared until I needed one.

As many of you can attest, nothing will bring you to the end of yourself faster than a sick or special needs child. This was the journey on which the Lord saw fit to take my husband and me. And it worked. Entrusting us with this fragile human with severe cranial deformities and neurological damage forced us to see life through a different lens. Pretense was no longer an option. My heart couldn't have been more vulnerable.

Lots of time was wasted thinking and worrying and fearing the worst. I became acutely aware of my need for Jesus. Suddenly, I couldn't get to Him fast enough. No fancy prayers were involved. I cried out to Him and pleaded with raw, often unintelligible words that resembled, *Please, Lord. Just please.*

I imagine the royal official's plea didn't sound much different. When he asked for help, Jesus gave a seemingly off-topic response. He said, "Unless you people see miraculous signs and wonders, you will never believe." But Jesus wasn't speaking to the royal official. He was addressing the crowd that had gathered around them. They wanted to see if Jesus would do the same signs and wonders He did in Jerusalem.

They were just curious, not desperate. Incidentally, they didn't see any miracles that day.

But guess who did.

Jesus told the royal official to go home and that his son would live. He took Jesus at His word and departed. That's it. That's how it went down. And that's exactly what all of us desperate people are supposed to do: Take. Jesus. At. His. Word.

Did Jesus heal my daughter instantaneously? No. But He never told me He would. Instead, He miraculously healed her over the course of several years, touching many lives in the process—namely mine. It kept me vulnerable and on my knees, which caused me to do the most unconventionally beautiful thing of all: surrender my life to Jesus and learn to take Him at His word.

PRAYER FOCUS

Thank God for His sovereign mercy and that He weaves desperation into our stories. Ask Him to increase your faith and help you to take Him at His word. Praise Him for being your comfort and your healer and for meeting you when you are most vulnerable.

MOVING FORWARD

o   Do you really know Jesus, or have you only heard about what He can do? Do you struggle to take Him at His word?

o   How has desperation driven you to Him? What were the circumstances? How did Jesus respond?

o Psalm 34:18 says, "The Lord is near to the broken-hearted and saves the crushed in spirit." How does knowing He's near in desperate times change the way we experience them?

RIDDLES

When [Jesus] was alone, those around him with
the twelve asked him about the parables. And he said
to them, "To you has been given the secret of the
kingdom of God, but for those outside everything is in
parables so that, 'they may indeed see but not perceive,
and may indeed hear but not understand, lest they
should turn and be forgiven.'"

MARK 4:10–12

Jesus, the disciples, and a small group of followers had
retreated from the larger crowd. With their teacher all to
themselves, it was the perfect time to ask questions—but Jesus'
answer just created more questions because He told them He
was speaking in parables so that some *wouldn't* understand
what He was saying.

Ummm, what now? Why would Jesus want some people
to *not* understand? That sounds completely off brand since
Jesus came to seek and save, not to corral and confound.

Makes it seem like He was speaking in riddles, not parables, and it doesn't at all jive with the other thing He said: "Ask, and it will be given to you; seek, and you will find; knock, and it will be opened to you. For everyone who asks receives, and the one who seeks finds, and to the one who knocks it will be opened" (Matthew 7:7–8).

Or…does it *totally* jive?

The disciples were seekers. They were so convinced Jesus was the Messiah, they left their lives to follow Him and become His students. They were in training to someday go out and do what He was doing—to teach and heal and lead more people to Him. But for now, they were sitting with Him apart from the crowd, asking difficult questions and working hard to understand His answers, observing His manner, and pondering all they were witnessing; all the while, the seeds of their faith were taking deep root in their hearts and minds.

Contemplation like that has a way of sifting true seekers from the looky-loos. People were flocking to Jesus every day because of what He could do for them. They wanted the immediate gratification of healing, either for themselves or their loved ones or just to witness something cool. And they wanted the miracle-man to deliver them from the Roman occupation, along with all the hardship that came with it. So when Jesus told stories instead, especially stories that were difficult to understand, the crowds got smaller.

Ironically, immediate gratification also separates true seekers from the less than sincere because when people *do* get what they want, they tend to move on. Once the blind could see, the lame could walk, and the show was over, the crowds got smaller still.

Maybe that was the point. Maybe Jesus cared more about the quality of discipleship than the quantity of disciples. The ones who stayed beyond the miracles, the ones who asked questions and wrestled through their confusion and doubt, to them He offered *the secret of the kingdom of God*—i.e., the ability to see with spiritual eyes and to understand the truth that Jesus is the Son of God through whom we have salvation; that He is life. Slowing down, chewing on and wrestling with profound and eternal things, trains us in the art of expectancy, making us ready for the revelation that comes from God, in His time and in His perfect way. And then the eyes and ears of our hearts are opened, and the parables cease to be riddles.

PRAYER FOCUS

Pray that God would give you more wisdom and discernment to understand His Word. And ask for patience to wait on Him as he faithfully reveals His truth in His time.

MOVING FORWARD

o   Read John 3:16. Describe God's heart for people. Whom did He send His Son for and why?

o   In what ways are you like the looky-loos?

o   What needs to change in your time with Jesus in order for you to lean in even more, the way the disciples did?

There.
We Said It.

Being a Jesus follower doesn't mean automatically understanding everything in the Bible—some things take time to work through and digest. It also doesn't mean automatically *liking* everything the Bible says—some things take time to wrestle with and ultimately submit to. In the spirit of authenticity and the desire to forge ahead, we're gonna say some things that aren't often said in church. In other words, we're gonna (1) wrestle out loud as we (2) seek to understand because we desire to (3) follow Jesus well.

SALT AND LIGHT. AND JOY.

"You are the salt of the earth, but if salt has lost its taste, how shall its saltiness be restored? It is no longer good for anything except to be thrown out and trampled under people's feet. "You are the light of the world. A city set on a hill cannot be hidden. Nor do people light a lamp and put it under a basket, but on a stand, and it gives light to all in the house. In the same way, let your light shine before others, so that they may see your good works and give glory to your Father who is in heaven."

MATTHEW 5:13–16

We don't always immediately understand the things Jesus said.

There. We said it.

And this seemingly random pairing of elements is no exception.

So why the two things—salt and light? Well, both serve a singular primary purpose. Salt serves the purpose of taste. Interesting only to those who like science (which we don't, but whatever), salt is an extremely stable compound and doesn't actually lose its saltiness. Salt is always salt. That is, unless it's immersed in and diluted with a large amount of water. And light serves the primary purpose of seeing. The unaided human eye can detect a light source as small as the flame of a candle from up to one and one-half miles away (more science). Which means light is extremely difficult to hide the brighter it is—unless it's covered or snuffed out entirely.

All that is to say that when salt has no taste and light can't be seen, they are worthless.

Jesus said His followers are to be salt and light, but more on that in a sec because that's not all He said. In Matthew 5, Jesus was preaching a longer sermon that included an important preamble to His analogy of salt and light: "Blessed are you when others revile you and persecute you and utter all kinds of evil against you falsely on my account. Rejoice and be glad, for your reward is great in heaven, for so they persecuted the prophets who were before you. You are the salt of the earth" (Matthew 5:11–13).

In context, it's our *response* to the awfulness of other people that is supposed to emulate the qualities of salt and light. We're supposed to be different. Flavorful. Light-giving. Instead of responding in kind, we're supposed to *be* kind. More than that, we're supposed to count ourselves blessed, to rejoice, and to be glad—because when we're mistreated for our faith, it means we're not hiding it under a proverbial basket. The prophets didn't hide their faith; they were outspoken and faith-filled and willing to follow God in less than ideal circumstances. Their words and deeds were flavorful and counter to the culture. They shined their light for all to see, which meant mistreatment came with the territory.

Being kind, joyful, and peace-filled because we're heaven bound is absolutely counter-culture. The typical response to insults and persecution is to hurl them back, to look out for #1, to demand respect and never settle for second best, to get defensive or pouty, to "speak our truth" especially when we sit behind a keyboard saying things we'd never say to someone's face. Just as salt's flavor is diluted by water, our faith and resolve to live by it is diluted by the world we live in.

But as followers of Jesus, we're supposed to be different in all the wonderful ways He was different. His words were humble, interesting, substantial, and timelessly true. Two thousand years later, they haven't lost their flavor. And His qualities still shine like the sun. People are drawn to Him just like we're drawn out of darkness by light. He loved people, He prayed for those who persecuted Him, and He ultimately died for the very people who mistreated Him. He was joy-filled because He knew what lay beyond the moment.

And we can be like Him.

PRAYER FOCUS

Ask God to reveal the ways you've been behaving more like the culture you live in than like Jesus, allowing your effectiveness for Him to be diluted and your hope hidden. Ask Him to give you the wisdom and resolve to be saltier and more light-giving.

MOVING FORWARD

o In what ways have you allowed yourself to become less salty? In what ways have you hidden your light under a basket?

o Sometimes Christians mistake "saltiness" for being harsh. But Jesus linked being salty to responding in joy and love. In your own words, explain why.

o Can you think of one way or one specific person to whom you can be flavorful and light-giving today?

LOVE

"You have heard that it was said, 'You shall love your neighbor and hate your enemy.' But I say to you, Love your enemies and pray for those who persecute you, so that you may be sons [and daughters] of your Father who is in heaven. For he makes his sun rise on the evil and on the good, and sends rain on the just and on the unjust…
You therefore must be perfect,
as your heavenly Father is perfect."

MATTHEW 5:43–48

Uffdah.

There. We said it.

Loving everyone, including your enemy, is a really beautiful-sounding idea. That is, until you have an enemy. Then it sounds nuts and downright impossible. Also impossible? To *be perfect like your Father in heaven*.

Spoiler alert: God knows we'll never be perfect this side of heaven. So why on earth did Jesus say it? And why did He waste His breath on such a lofty, unrealistic mandate like "love your enemies"?

Well first of all, we don't have to look very far to know what *not* loving looks like. Just turn on the news to see how political enemies behave. The horrible behavior and "dialogue" is everywhere you look, on both sides of the aisle, which is no doubt one of the many reasons Jesus didn't bother with politics—He didn't take sides because He's on His own side.

It's not just politics that puts humanity's broken brand of love on display. There are Twitter trolls, cyberbullies, and cancel-culture warriors. There are feuds that land in divorce court, family court, probate court, civil court, and criminal court (like the Hatfields and McCoys without the hats). There are protest parades and boycotts, infighting and backstabbing, school shootings and prison sentences, class warfare and actual warfare. There's little compromise, no forgiveness, lots of paranoia, and far too much estrangement because we keep the proverbial chip on our shoulder, we give the brush off, and we get stuff stuck in our craw.

And while it might feel good to lick our wounds and engage our bitterness, our way of loving and hating doesn't work. We're collectively miserable. We literally make ourselves sick with anger and hate—panic attacks, heart attacks, insomnia, ulcers, chronic pain in our backs and necks where we carry all of our stress and unresolved feelings. Our brows spend a ton of time furrowed, and we gift ourselves permanent frown lines, and for what? Nothing good comes from hate. Whatever momentary self-satisfaction we experience when we entertain it leaves behind darkness and a hardness of heart—like cement that begins to cure while we're standing in it up to our knees.

Considering our options, perhaps Jesus' command to love our enemies is as much for our own sake as theirs. Because love moves us forward—out of the pain, hurt, loss, or selfishness that got us stuck there in the first place.

So how do we love our enemies the way God loves his?

One way: Jesus.

"I can do all things through [Christ] who strengthens me" (Philippians 4:13).

It is, in fact, too lofty a virtue for us to love our enemies. Apart from Jesus, we're simply not capable of sustaining such grace-filled, self-effacing, self-denying behavior. Even if we choose kindness momentarily, eventually the moment ends, and we're left with the hate we began with.

But God's resources are endless—He never runs out of patience and mercy, never tires of doing good, never ceases to pursue us, forgive us, and lead us to greener pastures. And here's the really cool part: when we agree Jesus died on the cross to forgive us from sin and rose again victorious over that sin and all its consequences, the Holy Spirit then indwells us. Meaning, God lives in us, changing us and loving others in His impossible and perfect way *through* us.

In our own strength, we'll never truly love our enemies. And on this side of heaven, we'll never be perfect the way God is perfect. But we're in the process of being made perfect because God is transforming us into the image of His Son, the One who's perfect already. The One whose love has no boundaries and no end. The One whose sacrifice on the cross made it possible for us to know Him more and more. And the One we'll spend eternity with, our earthly sinfulness gone, surrounded by the people we helped love into heaven. Maybe even our enemies.

Uffdah.

PRAYER FOCUS

Pray that God will reveal any hate you've allowed to remain in your heart. Pray for the people who are hard for you to love. Ask God to make you more like Jesus, allowing you to love the unlovable for His sake and for His kingdom.

MOVING FORWARD

Loving our enemies doesn't automatically mean being friends with them. Some people are toxic. Some people are abusive, and we simply can't be in relationship with them for the sake of our physical or emotional safety. Some people harbor their own bitterness and wouldn't want a restored relationship even if we offered it to them. Some people have died, and nothing can be said or done—at least in this life. But regardless of your physical proximity to someone, Jesus wants your heart to remain soft and compassionate—which is possible when Jesus has your heart.

o   Who do you struggle to love and why?

o   What is God saying to you about your heart?

o   Read 1 John 4:7–8. What is one thing God wants you to
    do today that will make it obvious to others that you are
    a lot like your Father in heaven?

PRAYER

"Pray then like this: 'Our Father in heaven, hallowed
be your name. Your kingdom come, your will be done, on
earth as it is in heaven. Give us this day our daily bread,
and forgive us our debts, as we also have forgiven our
debtors. And lead us not into temptation,
but deliver us from evil.'"

MATTHEW 6:9–13

Praying sometimes feels like a one-way conversation. A
sometimes boring, I-can't-think-of-anything-good-to-say,
one-way conversation.

There. We said it.

In a world where we text because it's faster than actually
talking to someone, meaningful, connective conversations
are becoming less frequent. So is slowing down, getting quiet,
and waiting to hear what God has to say. And not even to
hear as we traditionally do with our outer ears—that would

be much easier—but to understand with an inner ear we often don't even know how to use.

In Matthew 6, Jesus was preaching a sermon with a lot of course corrections, the topics ranging from love to lust to divorce to revenge to money—to prayer. He began by telling the people what *not* to do: specifically, don't pray in order to be heard and admired by others, and don't fill your prayers with empty phrases and many words. Instead, "go into your room and shut your door and pray to your Father who is in secret" (Matthew 6:6). And that makes perfect sense because prayer is intended to be an intimate two-way conversation with God, not a liturgic public show. Of course, there's nothing wrong with praying corporately in church or with small groups of people—we can and should talk to God with others, praying for each other and worshiping Him together. That's church. "For where two or three are gathered in my name, there am I among them" (Matthew 18:20).

But corporate prayer shouldn't replace more intimate conversation with God. And while adjusting *where* you pray is fairly straightforward and simple, adjusting the empty words part—that's more difficult, because the truth is, we totally do that.

We know we're supposed to pray, and so we do. But we don't always know what to say, and we certainly don't like the stillness that comes in a quiet room when we run out of words. So we fill the empty space with many words. On the upside, spewing keeps us kneeling. It also keeps us from falling asleep, which is easier to do the older we get (seclusion + quiet = nap). And ultimately it feels pretty good to check "time with God" off our list of things to do. But that's not what prayer was designed to be because talking to God (or anyone else, for that matter) consists of two things: meaningful words *and* listening.

In His kindness, Jesus didn't just teach us what not to do or say. He also gave us a template for what our words *should* be. He didn't want us to be confused or discouraged or bewildered; He wants us to enter God's presence with confidence and the comfort that comes from knowing we're wanted. He also knew we would carry a lot of things into prayer—our worries, our fear, our love for Him, our brokenness, our thankfulness, our sin, our shame. We carry it all, all the time. In fact, sometimes the things we carry keep us so preoccupied, we fail to hand them over to the One who can actually help and heal us. So Jesus' prayer template wasn't meant to be strict or rigid; on the contrary, it's a guide that ushers us into the presence of God. It gives us space to say all the things we want to say, and all the things we should say:

– "Our Father in heaven"

> *My Father, who is on His throne in heaven,*
> *ruling, seeing, all-knowing, all-loving, holding*
> *everything together with your words…*

– "Hallowed be your name"

> *You are holy. You are King of the universe and*
> *set apart in my heart as Lord.*

– "Your kingdom come, your will be done"

> *Bring about your good plans, God. Multiply your*

kingdom in the hearts of men and women, and use me for your purposes. Your ways are higher and better than mine. Your ways are eternal in scope and intricate and beautiful beyond measure. Do your will, God, and let me see it and be amazed.

– "Give us this day our daily bread"

I pray for provision today, Lord. Would you direct my steps and give me faith and strength to follow you? Calm my heart—my needs are great—too many for me to meet and too overwhelming to face alone. Be faithful to your promise to provide, Lord. You know what I need, and because I'm seeking your kingdom, God, you must "add all these things to [me] as well." You've promised provision in Jesus' name. Thank you that you never lie or change.

– "And forgive us our debts, as we forgive our debtors"

Father, forgive me for being afraid all the time. Forgive me for doubting your faithfulness. Forgive me for persisting in greed and impatience and selfishness. Wipe my heart and mind clean, Lord, that I would again be pure like white snow. Make me like Jesus, the author and perfecter of my faith. And because of your great love for me and your forgiveness and grace, please help me to forgive others. Oh, that I would hold no

grudge or judgment, Lord, but that I would
extend grace as you do because of you and by
your power.

– "And lead us not into temptation, but deliver us
from evil."

Protect me going forward, Lord. Help me to see
the pitfalls, the lies from the enemy, along with
my safe passage out. You are good, God. I love
you. I serve you. I follow you. Amen.

It's a template, beautifully crafted by the author of prayer
Himself. And after saying words that are burden-lifting and
focus-shifting, it's time to listen for God to respond. In the
stillness. With patience. In expectancy that He will indeed
meet us in that place, holding up His end of the conversation.
Because out of His mercy and steadfastness and willingness to
bend low, He speaks through His Word, through our worship,
and to our inner ear. Oh, that we would remain awhile and
wait and believe He'll be faithful to make Himself known.

PRAYER FOCUS

This one should be easy, yeah?

MOVING FORWARD

o   How do you view prayer? As a boring or rigid or litur-
    gical practice? As an opportunity to give God your wish
    list before jumping back into your day? Or as a time to

pour your heart out to God in order for Him to pour Himself back into it?

o Why do you think Jesus taught about prayer with such specific instructions attached? What was His motive? His goal?

o What will you change about the way you pray moving forward? Where will you pray? When? How? Be intentional with this most precious relationship and protect it from becoming less than what God desires for it to be.

FASTING

They said to him, "The disciples of John fast often and offer prayers, and so do the disciples of the Pharisees, but yours eat and drink."

LUKE 5:33

Fasting is a bummer.

There. We said it.

Of course, fasting can also be a beautiful spiritual discipline—Jesus fasted. But eating is more enjoyable than not eating. Obviously. So understanding the purpose and place of fasting is important.

Jesus and His followers were different. John the Baptist's followers fasted and prayed often. The Pharisees' followers did too. And apparently everyone knew when everyone else was fasting and praying. But Jesus' followers were eating and drinking and clearly causing a raucous by breaking with religious norms. Perhaps the disciples were preoccupied by all the miracles; perhaps they were enthralled with the radically new things Jesus was teaching; perhaps they were barely keeping up with what they were witnessing and experiencing in His presence—so *not* eating didn't occur to them. But more on that in a sec.

First, here's what fasting isn't:

- Fasting isn't for public consumption, no pun intended. Fasting is like prayer in that we are not supposed to do it for the sake of people watching; it's not a way to earn spiritual street cred. In fact, the opposite it true: fasting is supposed to be private, between us and God. "And when you fast, do not look gloomy like the hypocrites, for they disfigure their faces that their fasting may be seen by others. Truly I say to you, they have received their reward. But when you fast, anoint your head and wash your face, that your fasting may not be seen by others but by your Father who is in secret. And your Father who sees in secret will reward you" (Matthew 6:16–18).

- Fasting isn't a way to pray harder. Sometimes we think we're contributing to the power of prayer—as though our passion, intensity, tears, or (in the case of fasting) self-discipline causes God to pay closer attention. But God is always paying close attention to His children. So while fasting might be evidence of our earnestness or need, it doesn't cause us to be more heard by God than when we're eating. "You know when I sit down and when I rise up; you discern my thoughts from afar…. Even before a word is on my tongue, behold, O Lord, you know it altogether" (Psalm 139:2, 4).

- Fasting isn't the end game; it's merely a means to an end. In other words, spiritual disciplines are only valuable if they usher us into the presence of God. In and of themselves, they're empty exercises. "For you [God] will not delight in sacrifice, or I would give it; you will not be pleased with a burnt offering. The sacrifices of God are a broken spirit; a broken and contrite heart, O God, you will not despise" (Psalm 51:16–17).

God wants our hearts, not our good or dutiful or penitent behavior. Fasting is a quiet act of faith. It is action born of the belief that what God gives is better than what the world gives—even food. It's an acknowledgement that the earth is sustained by the Bread of Heaven, the One who satisfies our souls in the way only He can. Fasting is a way to practice putting our flesh aside to seek God—His wisdom, His guidance, His intervention; our hunger pains even act as a reminder to pray. And fasting is a way to posture our hearts, open our hands, and abide in the presence of God.

Which is why the disciples were *not* fasting. They

were already in the presence of God in the flesh, spending every minute of every day with the One whom others were fasting to be near. Of course they weren't abstaining; they were partaking! They were following Him with their hearts postured to learn, their hands open to receive, their lives offered to Him the same way we now offer ours.

So whether we quietly fast or we eat and drink, our desire and aim should be the same: more of Jesus and what He gives.

PRAYER FOCUS

Ask God to reveal any misguided thinking you have in regard to the practice of your faith, and ask Him to show you how to truly posture your heart to learn and receive more from Him each day.

MOVING FORWARD

o What spiritual disciplines do you practice and why do you practice them?

o In what ways have you misunderstood disciplines like fasting, tithing, praying, and attending church?

o What is something that, if you fasted from it, would result in emptiness you could fill with more time with God?

TREASURE

"Lay up for yourselves treasure in heaven,
where neither moth nor rust destroys and where thieves
do not break in and steal. For where your treasure is,
there your heart will be also."

MATTHEW 6:20–21

We like money.

There. We said it.

Money makes life easier because it allows us to have things we value, like present-day stability and future-days security. It provides a measure of peace, comfort, and fun, and the ability to provide those things for others. Money allows us to solve a lot of problems with greater ease, so when we have it, we also have a greater degree of control over our lives.

Ish.

Because while money legitimately does all of those things, it's also fleeting. Stock markets crash. Jobs change or can be lost altogether. Property values fall. The cost of living soars. Cars, along with the teenagers driving them, are unpredictable, while rising taxes are not at all unpredictable. And if you suddenly have a lot of medical bills? Well those can scorch the earth.

Right after Jesus said, "Your Father who sees [you fasting] in secret will reward you," (Matthew 6:18), He explained how those rewards actually pile up in heaven as treasure—think wooden chest, gold coins, jewels. Of course, we don't actually know what our heavenly treasure will look like, and in God's house we'll have no need, nor will we care about riches once we've seen His face. Yet we're told throughout Scripture to lay up treasure in heaven, to store up (1 Timothy 6:17–19), to give here in order to have there (Luke 18:22), to be motivated by the rewards God promises (Revelation 22:12).

Continually we're told to add to our treasure in heaven instead of piling up treasure here. Why? Because this world is too unpredictable to ever actually offer security, and nothing we collect while we're in it is gonna cross the border into heaven anyway. As the metaphor goes: if you were traveling in another country and you knew customs wasn't going to allow any souvenirs to travel back home with you, would you spend your time shopping? Would you stuff your luggage full of new things you knew the border patrol would remove and trash? Or would you instead invest your treasure in your permanent home?

Interestingly, Jesus doesn't say we shouldn't be savers— but He's strongly recommending the bank where we should invest. He's actually appealing to our desire for security, our longing for nice things, our sense of "an honest day's work equals an honest day's pay," because He knows we're motivated by such things. We're motivated by the prize. But He's redirecting our efforts and lifting our eyes to heaven. He's teaching us what and where the prize actually is, and that it's tangible and measurable and incorruptible. And when eternity becomes the focus of our eyes and our minds, our hearts follow. Meaning, instead of being in love with a dying world and all the things in it (that don't satisfy us *ever*, by the way), we fall more deeply in love with Jesus, the people He loves, and our future home.

"For where your treasure is, there your heart will be also" (Matthew 6:21).

Money is necessary to live and whatnot; it's a tool to be used and one God provides in the here and now, so we should be thankful for whatever measure He gives. But that's all money is. It's temporary just like our bodies. And like our bodies, it's not gonna make it across the heavenly border. But the treasure we store away by following Jesus now—His kindness, humility, generosity, obedience, and faithfulness— the Father Himself will give back to us in heaven.

Cha-ching.

PRAYER FOCUS

Ask God to forgive you for sometimes loving money more than you love Him. Ask Him to retrain your eyes, to be thankful for what He provides in this world but also to be excited and hope-filled about your future home in heaven with Him. Cuz it's gonna be awesome.

MOVING FORWARD

o "For where your treasure is, there your heart will be also" (Matthew 6:21). Where's your treasure and why? Be honest with yourself.

o Read 1 Timothy 6:10. In your own words, explain Timothy's warning to rich people and poor people and everyone in between.

o In what ways can you store up more treasure in heaven today? What is God putting on your heart to do or say or pray that will add to your eternal riches?

ANXIETY

"Do not be anxious, saying, 'What shall we eat?' or 'What shall we drink?' or 'What shall we wear?' For the Gentiles seek after all these things, and your heavenly Father knows that you need them all. But seek first the kingdom of God and his righteousness, and all these things will be added to you. Therefore do not be anxious about tomorrow, for tomorrow will be anxious for itself. Sufficient for the day is its own trouble."

MATTHEW 6:31–34

Not being anxious is not always possible.

There. We said it.

Worry seems unavoidable since things often go wrong, and the consequences of things going wrong can be, well, bad. So not worrying seems unrealistic. *And* sometimes worrying causes us to take action, preventing the thing we worried about from happening at all—so worrying almost seems like the responsible thing to do (right?).

Yet of all the things Jesus could've talked about on this particular occasion, He chose to include worry and its natural consequence: anxiety. And lucky for twenty-first-century us He did, because we're obsessed with the topic.

Anxiety is on the rise, which is surprising since the world is actually healthier, safer, and more technologically advanced than ever before. Life spans are longer because of advancements in science and medicine and our overall understanding of wellness. Information flows freely around the globe, along with all the access, opportunity, and accountability it brings. People have the tools to be connected to one another in ways the ancient world couldn't have imagined—we text, snap, and video chat even the most mundane moments, which means we have the ability to engage with others whenever we choose.

And yet worry, fear, and anxiety are on the uptick in measurable ways, and our youngest generations seem to be the most affected—or at least they're the most frequently diagnosed (and the most enabled, but we digress). From social phobias to eating disorders, from panic attacks to the demand for safe spaces, from public shaming on Twitter to the normalization of narcissism (#selfcare), from the rise in prescribed pharmaceuticals to the always available recreational drugs on the street corner—

We're a mess because none of the ways we deal with worry, anxiety, and fear are working.

Truth is, there's nothing new under the sun. We may have our own dysfunctional ways of coping and our own unique triggers (and also the word "trigger"), but humanity has always struggled with anxiety—it was no different in Jesus' day. And worry has always been a blob monster, slowly and relentlessly engulfing everything it touches.

> "Look at the birds of the air: they neither sow nor reap nor gather into barns, and yet your heavenly Father feeds them. Are you not of more value than they? *And which of you by being anxious can add a single hour to his span of life?* And why are you anxious about clothing? Consider the lilies of the field, how they grow: they neither toil nor spin, yet I tell you, even Solomon in all his glory was not arrayed like one of these. But if God so clothes the grass of the field, which today is alive and tomorrow is thrown into the oven, will he not much more clothe you, O you of little faith?" (Matthew 6:26–30, emphasis added)

At first glance, Jesus' anxiety-remedy sounds too simple to work. And if all He said was "don't be anxious," it would indeed be impossible. But He explains the why and the how. And the who.

God, in His infinite ability, attentiveness, and love for creation, knows our needs already. He *knows*. Therefore, we can stop worrying about the things God already knows and seek Him instead—His kingdom, His heart, His priorities. Because when we do, God faithfully provides all the things we need. When we focus on His priorities and not our own, anxiety fades. Period.

The remedy for anxiety *is* simple, but that doesn't mean it's easy. It takes a disciplined mind to take worrisome thoughts captive and to make those thoughts obedient to the truth of who God is and what He promises to do. It takes spending time with Him to know Him more, to trust Him more, and to grow in the kind of faith that overshadows fear. It takes time reading our Bible in order to know what it says, in order to believe what it says. Because only in God and His Word will we find the peace and freedom from anxiety our overactive minds and hearts are longing for.

PRAYER FOCUS

Pour your heart out to God about the things you fear. He wants you to be honest with Him. But then thank Him for His promise to take care of you and replace some of your anxious thoughts with Scripture.

MOVING FORWARD

o   What makes you anxious and why?

o   Read Joshua 1:9. How does God's promise to provide for your needs, along with His promise to be "with you wherever you go," affect your anxious heart?

o   What are practical ways you can take your anxious and fearful thoughts captive, making them obedient to the truth of God's promises?

LOGS

"Why do you see the speck that is in your brother's eye,
but do not notice the log that is in your own eye?
Or how can you say to your brother, 'Let me take the
speck out of your eye,' while there is the log in your own
eye? You hypocrite, first take the log out of your own eye,
and then you will see clearly to take the speck out
of your brother's eye."

MATTHEW 7:3–5

I (Amanda) have a friend whose sin ended him. I mean, he's not dead or anything. But he didn't course correct when he desperately needed to, and it ruined his life. He didn't see his sin for what it was, didn't see the terrible, destructive, Paul Bunyan-sized log in his eye.

Watching it happen was painful, and not just because I cared about him and his family, and not just because his sin affected my own family. But it was also painful because God kept taking me back to Matthew 7:3–5. I could see my friend's sin so clearly. I could see that he needed to hate his sin more and justify it less, to grieve it and to repent of it completely and to a lot of people. And I could see the freight train of consequences barreling toward him at full speed.

But my own log? Well that was less interesting—at least to me.

Now back to him.

It became commonplace during that season of life to ruminate on what I was watching unfold. To replay moments that bewildered me, to wonder how long God would allow the behavior to continue, and to let my own woundedness fester. It was easy to judge him, easy to be frustrated with him, and easy to feel good about the person I wasn't—I wasn't him. I wasn't guilty of *that*. I wasn't guilty of not seeing such a gigantic log in my own eye.

What of my own log, you ask? Oh yeah, forgive me, Lord.

Now back to him.

It's funny how our prayers can wander. I somehow go from confessing my own sin to focusing on another person's sin to *Why the heck aren't you dealing with the forest in that person's eye, Lord?* in a matter of seconds. But it's also not funny at all because the more time I spend on someone else's sin, the less time I spend repenting of my own. And then my sin remains. And grows.

Sin takes ground. Unlike our justifying minds would have us believe, sin doesn't stay in its corner; it's not content to feed on crumbs. Pride grows. Self-righteousness grows. Bitterness grows. Materialism and greed and vanity and jealousy and insecurity and malice (my personal log list)—they all increase when they're allowed to stick around, because while we minimize our own sin's impact, it's on the move.

And the result is just gross.

> [Jesus] also told this parable to some who trusted in themselves that they were righteous, and treated others with contempt: "Two men went up into the temple to pray, one a Pharisee and the other a tax collector. The Pharisee, standing by himself, prayed thus: 'God, I thank you that I am not like other men, extortioners, unjust, adulterers, or even like this tax collector. I fast twice a week; I give tithes of all that I get.' But the tax collector, standing far off, would not even lift up his eyes to heaven, but beat his breast, saying, 'God, be merciful to me, a sinner!'
>
> "I tell you, this man went down to his house [forgiven], rather than the other. For everyone who exalts himself will be humbled, but the one who humbles himself will be exalted." (Luke 18:9–14)

Jesus warns us plainly: if we don't get low, if we don't see and deal with our own sin to the point of beating our breasts and crying to God for forgiveness and mercy, we will surely suffer the consequences.

Instead of allowing me to fixate on the sins of other

people, my loving Father keeps turning my head back to the mirror. Forcefully. Painfully. But always lovingly. Because God knows the havoc sin wreaks, and He's unwilling to surrender me to it. In recent months, God has changed the subject back to the log in my own eye again and again. *His mercies are new each morning* (Lamentations 3:22–23) because He's good and patient and faithful—and because I give Him plenty of messy material to work with. Which means there's just no time to sit in judgment of anyone else.

My friend's story is indeed a cautionary tale but not because he sinned.

Because he didn't see.

PRAYER FOCUS

Ask God to reveal your sin to you. Ask Him for forgiveness. Ask Him to help you stop judging others and thank Him for calling your sin out of the darkness and into His purifying, restorative light.

MOVING FORWARD

o What's distracting you from the log in your own eye?

o Read Psalm 139:23–24. What is God revealing to you about your heart?

o Removing logs is a daily job, not a one-and-done. What changes can you make today that would allow you to follow Jesus with unimpaired vision?

A NEW THING

John's disciples and the Pharisees were fasting. And people came and said to him, "Why do John's disciples and the disciples of the Pharisees fast, but your disciples do not fast?" And Jesus said to them, "Can the wedding guests fast while the bridegroom is with them? As long as they have the bridegroom with them, they cannot fast. The days will come when the bridegroom is taken away from them, and then they will fast in that day. No one sews a piece of unshrunk cloth on an old garment. If he does, the patch tears away from it, the new from the old, and a worse tear is made. And no one puts new wine into old wineskins. If he does, the wine will burst the skins—and the wine is destroyed, and so are the skins. But new wine is for fresh wineskins."

MARK 2:18–22

Let's reiterate. The Pharisees and their disciples fasted.

John the Baptist and his disciples fasted. Jesus and His disciples did not. The discrepancy was perplexing to some people, so they asked Jesus, "What gives? Why aren't you guys fasting?"

Since the inquiry was from "some people" and not the contentious teachers of the law, it was likely asked in earnest. Jesus must've thought so, anyway, because He answered with the following three (paraphrased) parables.

- Parable #1: There's a time and place for fasting, and now is not it. You fast once the groom leaves the wedding ceremony, not while everyone is still celebrating.

- Parable #2: Mending an old shirt with new fabric doesn't work. The new patch will shrink after washing and pull away from the shirt. Not only does that not fix anything, it makes it worse.

- Parable #3: Pouring new wine into old wineskins is a recipe for disaster. An old wineskin has already been stretched to capacity; it can't grow any more. If you fill it with new wine that ferments and expands, the skins will burst, and the wine will be wasted.

Presumably the people understood these illustrations a lot better than we do; nowadays, they require a little sleuthing because how many of us repair old clothes, select our own wine vessels, or fast over anything, least of all a groom? But in order for us to understand how these parables answer the why-isn't-Jesus-fasting question, we must first discern why the fasters were fasting.

John the Baptist, the final old covenant prophet, preached the sobering message of repentance. His fasting was of the Old Testament sackcloth-and-ashes variety, which was integrity driven and honorable. Some of the Pharisees, the unrepentant ones, were a bunch of big fat phonies looking to appear pious and righteous. They didn't have an honorable bone in their self-serving bodies.

So there were two different motives derived from two different systems. One was in compliance to old covenant convention; the other was manmade, hypocritical garbage. Jesus wasn't about either; hence He didn't fast on account of either. But Jesus is not anti-fasting, as we know. He fasted in the wilderness for forty days and exhorts His followers to fast in private as well (Matthew 5:18).

Different system. Different motive.

In plain English and to sum up, Jesus is using the parables to say, "Look, this isn't about what my disciples are doing, fasting or otherwise. It's about what I'm doing. And I'm doing something new. My new thing doesn't mix with the old. So relax, my guys will fast when I'm gone, but while I'm here, we're going to eat and celebrate my awesome new thing."

That awesome new thing = 100 percent Jesus. Trying to patch up old-school dogma or self-righteous rule following with a little bit of Jesus will only tear things to shreds. Jesus can't be stitched over a works-based religion. His grace can't be poured into a vintage, legalistic container. Jesus bursts that nonsense wide open! He is all about the new. The new thing only He can do in the new creations that can only be found in Him.

PRAYER FOCUS

Ask God to reveal what things you're doing with wrong motives. Pray that He'll burst any extra rules or legalism wide open and fill you with His grace and all things new.

MOVING FORWARD

o Jesus fasted in private but not in public. Explain why you think that is.

o Religious tradition is still alive and well. Are your actions motivated more by church practice and tradition or by celebrating Jesus' awesome new thing?

o We can't patch up our old lives with a little bit of Jesus. It's all or nothing. One hundred percent Jesus = a brand new us. What old thing do you need to let go of in order to surrender to the new?

LIGHT SOURCE

Again Jesus spoke to them, saying, "I am the light of the
world. Whoever follows me will not walk in darkness,
but will have the light of life."

JOHN 8:12

For a landscape painting to make sense, an artist must
first evaluate the light source. The sun illuminates the objects
and determines the angle of the shadows. When the nature
of it is misrepresented, the whole composition gets screwy.
For instance, the shadows from a picket fence can't crisscross
all over each other. They should be in alignment. Everything
that reflects the light responds accordingly. And if that's not
happening on the canvas, well, it's not the sun that got it
wrong.

Needless to say, the Pharisees were by and large a bunch
of hack religion painters making a total mess of the spiritual
landscape. While they were casting their shadows all over the
place, Jesus said: "I am the light of the world. Whoever follows

me will not walk in darkness, but will have the light of life" (John 8:12).

Light was a reoccurring theme in the Jewish tradition and was synonymous with direction and rescue. It was the light of God's presence that led their ancestors through the Exodus from Egypt as well as the wilderness. Light was a big deal. Jesus leveled up that claim by saying He is now the one and only light source synonymous with direction and rescue. But because they were directionless and rescue-averse, the Pharisees didn't even address His bold declaration. Instead, they honed in on a technicality.

Jesus just told them He's the *Light of the World*—aka God's manifest presence—and what were they miffed about? That He was appearing as His own witness. As in, "Yeah, so that's what you say, but who else is saying that? No one else is saying that you're the Light of the World, so it doesn't count. You don't get to be that." It was as imbecilic as telling the sun it needs a human witness to prove that it's shining.

All of the Pharisees' rhetorical nonsense was based on human understanding, which is exactly what Jesus pointed out. They had no clue with whom they were speaking or what the light-of-the-world-talk was about because they were groping around in the dark. "The light shines in the darkness, and the darkness did not comprehend it" (John 1:5 NASB).

They didn't have to keep groping, though; they very much had a choice. They could've stopped misrepresenting with their screwy compositions and evaluated the light source. They could've humbled themselves and asked for lessons instead of stubbornly pretending they were the masters. They could've pitched their messes in the trash and grabbed a new canvas.

That's the beauty of it all; the option is always there to start anew! Every day, in fact. Our Lord invites us to come out of the shadows, repent, and live as children of light (Ephesians 5:8). And when we do, Jesus illuminates the truth, and then our lives respond accordingly. Aligned with His Word, we become the masterpieces that reflect His perfect brilliance.

PRAYER FOCUS

Thank the Lord for giving you direction and rescuing you from darkness. Repent if you've been groping around in the dark trying to create your own life, your own masterpiece. Praise Him that His mercies are new every day and for the privilege of reflecting His light.

MOVING FORWARD

o   Do you see Jesus as synonymous with direction and rescue? In what way does your life reflect that?

o   Jesus revealed a giant truth, yet the Pharisees were stuck on a silly technicality. In your life, what lesser issues have hijacked the truths Jesus reveals?

o   Do you need to repent for misrepresenting the Light of the World? If so, in what ways can you grab another canvas and start over?

EXPOSED

Then all of the people of the surrounding country of the Gerasenes asked [Jesus] to depart from them, for they were seized with great fear. So he got into the boat and returned [to Galilee]. The man from whom the demons had gone begged that he might be with him, but Jesus sent him away, saying, "Return to your home, and declare how much God has done for you." And he went away, proclaiming throughout the whole city how much Jesus had done for him.

LUKE 8:37–39

Two totally different reactions to Jesus.

On the one hand, there was a man who was possessed by a legion of demons. A *legion*. The demons drove him from his home and family to live among tombs where he shrieked naked at all hours and was so dangerous and violent that no one dared even pass by (Luke 8:26–36). So…basically the things horror movies are made of.

He responded to Jesus by begging to go with Him.

On the other hand, there was a large group of people who were apparently more afraid of the guy who got rid of the demons than they'd been of the crazy-demon-horror-movie-man.

They begged Jesus to leave.

Which sounds so strange, but is it actually unique? Because, spoiler alert, Jesus was ultimately rejected and crucified by people who'd witnessed all kinds of miracles, not just this one. And He's continually rejected today, no matter how many Old Testament prophecies He fulfills (#miracles) or how many people testify to the supernatural difference He's made in their lives (#moremiracles). Some people want no part of Jesus—and why is that? No doubt there are unique reasons for each individual, but Jesus offered one overarching explanation. And it isn't flattering.

"And this is the judgment: the light has come into the world, but people loved the darkness rather than the light because their works were evil. For everyone who does wicked things hates the light and does not come to the light, lest his works should be exposed" (John 3:19–20).

As it turns out, there are different ways to fear. Jesus freed an entire region of people from a man who struck fear into their hearts, a man who couldn't be bound by chains. Yet the miracle Jesus performed also caused the people to be *seized with great fear*—because Jesus' light exposes more than just the worst among us. In other words, the possessed man wasn't the only one with issues, and Jesus' actions and their ramifications demanded a response the people weren't willing to give. They shrank from His light and begged Him to leave. And then they resumed their lives in the dark.

Funny how the person most desperate to remain with Jesus was the one whose mess was exposed already—the one who had no chance of hiding and nothing more to lose. Because while light exposes things we'd sometimes rather hide, when we step into it, we quickly discover that being near Jesus is the only place we want to be, warts and all. He sees our whole pitiful selves and rescues us from the sin that enslaves, making us safe and whole and new.

We're exposed by the light, that's true. But then we're changed by it.

PRAYER FOCUS

Spend some time praising Jesus for who He is, what He's done, and for His powerful and available saving grace. Then ask for courage to remain in His sin-exposing light.

MOVING FORWARD

o What parts of your heart or life do you work hard to hide?

o How do you respond to the light of Jesus? Do you shrink from it when you fail? Are you reluctant to give up the things that don't honor Him? Do you welcome Him even if it means exposure and change?

o In what ways can you pursue Jesus' presence more today?

TEST QUESTION

Lifting up his eyes, then, and seeing that a large crowd was coming toward him, Jesus said to Philip, "Where are we to buy bread, so that these people may eat?" He said this to test him, for he himself knew what he would do.

JOHN 6:5–6

Some people don't test well. They're more tactile learners. Philip was one of those people.

As soon as Jesus asked Him where they could get bread for a gathering of more than five thousand people, Philip went into logistics mode. They were only a few miles outside of his hometown, Bethsaida. So no doubt, he racked his brain wondering where he could go and how he could make this thing happen. Duh, he couldn't and finally concluded as much. He reported to Jesus that it would take more than half a year's wages to buy enough bread for each person to have a bite.

Oh Philip.

This wasn't week one. He'd already seen plenty of miracles, hundreds maybe. At the very least, Philip should've known that when Jesus asks a question, it's not because He's the one who needs to hear the answer. Jesus didn't expect Philip to know exactly what He was about to do. How could he? He was testing Philip to see if his thinking was in the same stratosphere. Was Philip going to evaluate the situation naturally or look to the One who could fix it supernaturally? Would his answer involve faith and Jesus or a calculator and a gold card?

To get a real-time reading on our faith, Jesus knows exactly which question to ask in exactly the right circumstance—and this was the perfect scenario to test Philip. Had Jesus asked him how a leper could be healed or how a blind man's sight could be restored, Philip would've readily answered, "Only you can do that, Jesus." Although correct, it would've been a throwaway response. Those miracles required nothing of Philip, not even faith. Jesus knew to test Philip with a seemingly natural, albeit logically impossible, predicament. And Philip didn't do so great. His math problem exposed his faith problem, which was exactly the point.

I'm sure most of us can relate to Philip. We marvel at who Jesus is and what He can do, but as soon as He asks us to participate in a miracle, we immediately go into logistics mode and start crunching the numbers. Often our conclusion isn't any better than Philip's. Consequently, our prayers reflect our lack of faith and become little more than grim reports derived from human assessment. *I did the math, Lord, and half a year's wages won't cover this college tuition or these medical bills or a multi-season series about the life of Christ.*

Oh modern-day Philips.

The question is a test, and the test is an invitation. It's an opportunity to shift our focus from what we can't do to what He is going to do. Jesus didn't ask Philip, "Where are *you* going to get the bread?" He asked, "Where are *we* going to get the bread?" Jesus already had a plan. He knew how it would all go down. He was inviting Philip to jump into the same stratosphere, put down his silly calculator, hold out his empty hands, and watch Jesus do impossible math.

PRAYER FOCUS

Ask God to increase your faith so that your answers always involve Him. Praise Him for testing you and inviting you to participate in what He's already doing. Give Him all the glory for doing impossible math on your behalf.

MOVING FORWARD

o What is your default? Do you tend to evaluate impossible situations (e.g., financial debt, medical report, prodigal loved ones) naturally, or do you look to the One who can fix things supernaturally?

o Describe a time when you knew the Lord was testing you. How did you do? What was the result?

o God already has a plan. What current impossible situation is He inviting you to participate in?

TEST ANSWER

Jesus called the disciples to him and said, "I have compassion for these people; they have already been with me three days and have nothing to eat. I do not want to send them away hungry, or they may collapse on the way." His disciples answered, "Where could we get enough bread in this remote place to feed such a crowd?"

MATTHEW 15:32–33 NIV

The first time around, the logistical assessment was somewhat understandable; it was a new situation. Philip was tested, Jesus performed a miracle, and perhaps they all had a good laugh at the mistake while everyone learned a valuable lesson. Except they didn't because the second time it happened, every last disciple failed miserably.

Once again, they were in a remote area with a massive crowd of hungry people, four thousand this time instead of five. Jesus told the disciples He wanted everyone to eat before sending them home.

If nothing else, it should've been a déjà vu moment. But it wasn't. Instead the disciples unwittingly asked Jesus the same question He had asked them the first time. "Where can we get bread in this remote place to feed such a crowd?" Clearly, theirs was not a test or an invitation, just an expression of genuine cluelessness.

Needless to say, the original feeding of the five thousand was not a small or quick miracle. It was an hours-long, systematized, interactive experience. The crowd assembled in groups prior to the bread and fish, Jesus multiplied the bread and fish, the disciples distributed the bread and fish, everyone ate the bread and fish, and the disciples gathered the leftover bread and fish. In other words, there was just no missing it. Yet there they stood asking Jesus where they could get bread in this remote place.

What on earth?

This would've been an appropriate time to tell the disciples how utterly ridiculous they were. Or how they were going to ruin everything if they didn't pull it together and start trusting Him with the impossible. Of course Jesus didn't do that. In lieu of a much deserved rebuke, He asked the disciples one simple question, "How many loaves do you have?" (v. 34). Once again, He calmly invited them to hand over their "not enough" so He could multiply it into more than what they need.

The only thing more staggering than the disciples' blanket amnesia and all-around abysmal failure is how patiently Jesus responded to it. He let them get it wrong then shifted the focus back to Him. Throughout each and every interaction, Jesus consistently demonstrated: This is how you do it, boys. This is how you respond.

Perhaps the feeding of the four thousand was less of a faith test and more of a ministry answer. Jesus' response was one of compassion but not just for the hungry crowd—for the learning disciples as well. He knew what these men would be up against. In the not so distant future, they, too, would be teaching and ministering to thousands of new converts. The calling on their lives would necessitate a Christ-like compassion for the hungry, tenderness for the broken, and an endless amount of patience for those who were struggling in their faith. None of that is possible without humility, and humility is born out of repeated failure. Just ask Peter.

Over and over again, Jesus lets the disciples get it wrong. Through hours-long interactive experiences, He taught them not only who to trust with impossible things but also how to respond to imperfect people so that they, in turn, could teach others how focus on Him.

Jesus knows exactly which question to ask in exactly the right circumstance. Sometimes it's to test, and other times it's to demonstrate. Either way, the answer always requires us to give Him what we have. Whether it's compassion, tenderness, patience, humility, or faith, our supply is never enough—that was the point of all the bread and fish multiplying. If we hand over the little bit that we have, Jesus will multiply it into more than we need.

PRAYER FOCUS

Thank God for His compassion and endless patience. Ask Him to continually teach you how to respond. Thank Him for taking your "not enough" and turning it into "more than you need."

MOVING FORWARD

o   What repeated failure has God used to shift your focus back to Him?

o   How has He shown you compassion in His response?

o   In what ways have your experiences with Jesus taught you to more effectively minister to others?

FOLLOWER

Then Jesus declared, "I am the bread of life. Whoever comes to me will never go hungry, and whoever believes in me will never be thirsty."

JOHN 6:35 NIV

Reporter: The backlash from Jesus' "Bread of Life" statement continues to polarize the region. Not surprisingly, His claims incensed those within the Sanhedrin, but they're also hitting close to home. Many households are now divided over Jesus and where following Him will actually lead. We have with us one of Jesus' followers to give us an idea of what's going on. Thank you for being willing to share your perspective. Let's start from the beginning. The first time you heard Jesus teach was the day before the infamous "Bread of Life" statement, on the mountainside near Bethsaida?

Follower: That's correct. My husband and I went thinking we'd only be there for a few hours. But we were amazed by His words and ended up staying the entire day. It was late, and we were hungry, but neither of us wanted to leave.

Reporter: And that's when Jesus multiplied the bread and fish?

Follower: Yes, it was like nothing we'd ever seen. Every person ate until they were full. I looked at my husband and said, "Surely, He is the prophet we have been expecting."

Reporter: And was your husband in agreement?

Follower: At the time, yes. He even sided with those who wanted to force Jesus to accept the kingship, though he sadly changed his mind the next day.

Reporter: I've heard many impassioned accounts about what happened that day. Incredibly, Jesus' statement about bread eclipsed His miracle of multiplying it. What happened?

Follower: The next morning, we found Jesus on the other side of the lake. There was already a crowd, and they were asking Him questions. He started talking to them about how they wanted food that spoils verses food that endures to eternal life.

Reporter: Do you think Jesus was suggesting that the only reason they were following Him was for more bread?

Follower: Yes, because the only reason most of them *were* following Him was for more bread. The crowd was annoyed when He refused to produce it. When He instead said, "I am the bread that came down from heaven," they grumbled.

Reporter: But not you?

Follower: I didn't care about food; I was hungry for His words. My heart was pounding as He spoke, like something powerful was drawing me to Him. At one point, someone asked Jesus, "What must we do, to be doing the works of God?" As soon as He said, "This is the work of God, that you believe in him whom he has sent" (John 6:28–29), I rejoiced. Because I do believe in Him.

Reporter: You believe that He is the Son of God sent from heaven? That He is the Bread of Life?

Follower: I do. He went on to explain that those who believe have eternal life, and whoever eats this bread will live forever. The bread is His flesh, which He will give for the life of the world (John 6:51).

Reporter: And that didn't offend you? I understand most of the crowd found those words to be shocking and reprehensible.

Follower: If taken literally, they would be. I agree it's a hard teaching, but it's not difficult to understand. I choose to accept that Jesus has come down from heaven to nourish us and give us eternal life.

Reporter: But your husband did not. How does he feel about your decision? And how might this affect your relationship?

Follower: Mostly he's concerned. But I'm glad he's still paying close attention because the truth will come out; that we can count on. As far as our relationship, we'll be okay. This story is far from over.

PRAYER FOCUS

Take a moment to pray for those who don't know the Bread of Life. Ask God for the opportunity to share who He is and what He came to do.

MOVING FORWARD

o   Is there a defining moment when you knew Jesus is exactly who He says He is? Describe it.

o   What did Jesus' words provoke among the crowd? What do they provoke in you?

o   Read 1 John 5:20. What aspects of Jesus' character are you eager to keep learning about so that you can understand and know Him more?

DESERTER

Jesus said to them, "Very truly I tell you, unless you eat the flesh of the Son of Man and drink his blood, you have no life in you…." On hearing it, many of his disciples said, "This is a hard teaching. Who can accept it?"

JOHN 6:53, 60–61 NIV

Reporter: I spoke with your wife earlier regarding your encounter with Jesus. As she continues to follow Him, you have chosen to turn back. Why?

Deserter: I wanted to believe. I thought finally our people would receive deliverance from the Roman oppression. My wife said to me, "Surely He is the prophet we've been expecting," and I agreed with her, especially after He fed the entire crowd.

Reporter: So you do concede that it was a miracle?

Deserter: Yes. We saw it with our own eyes. It's why we followed Him across the lake.

Reporter: There's a rumor circulating that the Pharisee Nicodemus admitted to Jesus that he believed Jesus was from God, that His miracles prove that. What would you say to that?

Deserter: I'd say you shouldn't circulate rumors.

Reporter: Fair enough, but do you not wonder about the purpose of the miracles or why Jesus is making such unorthodox claims?

Deserter: Look, I don't know the how or why. I just know we need a military king, not a talker going on about bread and a kingdom that is not of this world. Our people are suffering here and now. Many are hungry, and that's His answer, to eat Him? It's despicable.

Reporter: Is that what caused you to turn back? What He said about eating His flesh?

Deserter: Well yeah. Things got a little chaotic. Then Jesus asked if we were offended.

Reporter: Obviously you were.

Deserter: His teaching was absurd and in direct opposition to the law and prohibited by Moses. I can't believe my wife is still following Him. I can't believe any of this, really; I refuse to.

Reporter: Interesting choice of words. Isn't that the one thing Jesus said to do, "This is the work of God, that you believe in him whom he has sent" (John 6:29)?

Deserter: I won't. I don't care how many miracles He does. I just hope my wife doesn't get hurt in all of this. The truth is going to come out; that we can count on.

Reporter: That seems to be the only thing anyone can agree on these days. This story is far from over.

PRAYER FOCUS

Thank God for revealing hard truth to us. Ask Him for deeper understanding with verses that offend or confuse you. Praise Him for exceeding our expectations of who He is.

MOVING FORWARD

o   Take the time to read through John chapter 6. Which verses arrest your attention and why?

o   Why do you think so many people struggled with this teaching?

o   Describe in your own words why Jesus calls Himself the Bread of Life and what He meant when He said we must feed on Him.

THE DOGGONE TRUTH

Immediately a woman whose little daughter had an unclean spirit heard of him and came and fell down at his feet. Now the woman was a Gentile, a Syrophoenician by birth. And she begged him to cast the demon out of her daughter. And he said to her, "Let the children be fed first, for it is not right to take the children's bread and throw it to the dogs." But she answered him, "Yes, Lord; yet even the dogs under the table eat the children's crumbs." And he said to her, "For this statement you may go your way; the demon has left your daughter." And she went home and found the child lying in bed and the demon gone.

MARK 7:25–30

Sometimes there's a significant disconnect between a single moment in history and what that moment actually means in the context of history. And that's an important distinction because hearing Jesus basically compare a woman to a dog would otherwise be completely derailing. (Um, we're a little derailed.)

So here's the context.

News of Jesus had been spreading throughout the region and apparently all the way to Phoenicia, a Roman province of Syria also known as Canaan. A Syrophoenician woman (in other words, a not-Jewish woman) heard that Jesus was nearby, so she found Him and threw herself at His feet in the hope that He would heal her little girl.

It's a familiar scene that was repeated throughout the Gospels. Desperate parents came to Jesus with desperate pleas, and Jesus responded by healing their ailing children, which is exactly what happened here. Only this interaction included seemingly ungracious, unkind words.

Seemingly.

More context. Israel was God's chosen nation, which meant that since the creation of the world, God had been intentionally revealing Himself to them—His enduring love, His patience, His power to rescue, His mercy. Over and over again, the King of the universe offered them forgiveness and restored relationship with Him if only they would turn away from their sins and back to Him. The Old Testament is, in fact, the story of God's constant pursuit of the nation of Israel and their frequent rebellion against His love and laws.

And now we're catching up to the woman who probably knew very little about the God of Israel or Jewish tradition—though she had definitely heard something about Jesus. For that very reason, *she made her plea based on who He was, not based on who she was.*

She didn't argue with Jesus' assertion of her lowly status or that the Gentiles were supposed to be, at the moment, next in line for relationship with Him. She wasn't offended like we are when we read her story. In fact, she offered nothing but faith that He could do what she was asking Him to do. Which is exactly what He did, attributing His willingness to her great faith that persisted in spite of Him giving her every reason to give up. The process was painful, but she passed the test, especially the humility part.

Hers is the position we all should take before a Holy God—that we deserve nothing from Him because we are unclean and unworthy. We may not like the dog analogy, but in the presence of a Holy God, there are worse things we could be called, and our defensiveness is likely rooted in the same self-justification and surface-level good behavior that the religious leaders of her day clung to. Like them, we sometimes think we're better or more deserving than we actually are. Like them, we lack the humility required for real repentance.

More context. This moment in history serves the larger story God is telling, from creation to Jesus to someday revelation. Because while salvation came first to the Jews, it was on the move for the Gentiles. It wouldn't be long before Jesus would be put to death by His own people, the message of salvation *through Him* rejected. And then upon His resurrection and ascension, His followers would be sent to all people with the message of salvation for anyone who humbly believes.

Including the momma who, upon returning home, found her little girl set free.

PRAYER FOCUS

Persist in your prayer in spite of the occasional feeling that God is not considering it. And while you're at it, ask Him for more humility. Disclaimer: In His kindness, He will give it, which makes asking for humility a very brave thing to do.

MOVING FORWARD

o   What was your gut reaction to the way Jesus interacted with this woman and why?

o   Most of us are offended by Jesus' words, but according to Romans 6:23, what do we all actually deserve? (Hint, hint…instead of trying to level up, we all gotta be leveled down.)

o   Knowing that we're sinners saved by grace because of who Jesus is, not who we are, what role should humility play (1) in our posture before a Holy God, (2) in our level of gratitude, and (3) in our interaction with others?

UNDESERVED

A centurion had a servant who was sick and at the point of death, who was highly valued by him. When the centurion heard about Jesus, he sent to him elders of the Jews, asking him to come and heal his servant.

LUKE 7:2–3

Jesus healed a lot of people, but not one of them "deserved" it. Truth is, no amount of goodness entitles a person to healing—or anything else for that matter—though a group of Jewish elders thought otherwise. They tried to persuade Jesus to heal the centurion's servant on account of him being a decent enough guy. "He is worthy to have you do this for him, for he loves our nation, and he is the one who built us our synagogue" (Luke 7:4–5).

Their strategy made sense. Why bury the lede when appealing to a rabbi? Their entire religious structure had been distorted by a works-based merit system. And even though the centurion wasn't Jewish, the elders argued that he did God's work by proxy, thus making him worthy of a kickback.

To be fair, the Jewish elders did "plead earnestly," which means they genuinely cared about the centurion. So much so, they scrapped his humble petition and built a better case. They pleaded his case, talked him up, and Jesus responded. He agreed to go to the centurion's house. Undoubtedly, the elders were high-fiving each other all the way there.

Then the second batch of men came out. They relayed the centurion's actual message, and Jesus was amazed. He said He hadn't found such great faith, even in Israel. Mind you, the centurion wasn't there to receive the compliment. Jesus said it for everyone else's benefit—and specifically for the elders' benefit. He told the men who had supposedly dedicated their entire lives to God that it was the pagan Gentile who got it right. Not exactly a compliment or a thank you. No more high-fives.

That's the end of the story, so we don't know what the Jewish elders made of the whole situation. Either they were humbled by Jesus' words and repented, or they were offended and hated Him. Historically speaking, it was likely the latter, but just for fun, we'll give them the benefit of the doubt. Regardless, we can learn from their original self-righteous assumption and erroneous approach to Jesus.

Deserve is a complicated concept when it comes to faith. Had the centurion received what he truly deserved, he would've been incinerated on the spot. The same goes for the elders, the disciples, Mary, and every other human on the planet, including you and me. What we deserve is eternal separation from God. Thankfully, God does not treat us as we deserve or repay us according to our iniquities (Psalm 103:10). What we receive instead is a grace so amazing that Jesus is willing to do nice things for us, like let us live and allow us to ask Him for stuff.

Even so, our humanity kicks in, and that centurion-like humility can easily morph into elder-like pride. Rack up enough quiet times, church attendance, volunteering, small group participation, etc., and we can delude ourselves into thinking we deserve certain spiritual kickbacks. Our distorted merit system feels righted, secure. And we build our spiritual résumé hoping Jesus will give us favor.

That is self-righteousness, and that is what Jesus hates.

Instead, take your cues from the centurion and humbly ask for help because Jesus has more than proven Himself in the unmerited favor department. That is what He extended to the centurion that day: grace. That is what you and I have access to though Jesus' death and resurrection. And that is what saves us, heals us, and makes us whole.

Not us.

Only Jesus.

PRAYER FOCUS

Ask God to expose any self-righteous attitudes or sense of entitlement. Thank God for not giving you what you deserve and for the confidence to approach Him for grace.

MOVING FORWARD

o   Do you ever find yourself building a case for why Jesus should help you?

o   Is it hard to accept that our spiritual résumé is useless compared to God's grace? Why or why not?

o   We are called to approach God's throne of grace with confidence, not arrogance. Describe the difference.

AMAZING JESUS

The centurion sent friends, saying to him, "Lord, do not trouble yourself, for I am not worthy to have you come under my roof. Therefore I did not presume to come to you. But say the word, and let my servant be healed. For I too am a man set under authority, with soldiers under me: and I say to one, 'Go,' and he goes; and to another, 'Come,' and he comes; and to my servant, 'Do this,' and he does it." When Jesus heard these things, he marveled at him, and turning to the crowd that followed him, said, "I tell you, not even in Israel have I found such faith."

LUKE 7:6–9

Reporter: As far as compelling stories go, yours ticks all the boxes: drama, multi-dimensional characters, plot twists, and a satisfying outcome. Walk me through it. One of your servants whom you value highly was sick and about to die, so you…?

Centurion: I called for Jesus. Like everyone else in Capernaum, I heard about the wine at the wedding and the healing of the royal official's son.

Reporter: Okay, but let's not ignore the Roman elephant in the room. Not only are you are a pagan Gentile, as a centurion, you're an integral cog in the occupation machine.

Centurion: Yes, my job is to enforce Caesar's rule over the Jewish people. However, one doesn't have to be cruel to be effective.

Reporter: Be that as it may, you're still an oppressor of the Jewish people asking a Jewish rabbi for a massive favor. Is that why you sent a Jewish delegation in your stead?

Centurion: No. I sent them because I was wholly undeserving to be in the presence of Jesus.

Reporter: A humble centurion? Multi-dimensional character, indeed.

So Jesus agrees to help your servant. You see Him walking toward your house…and you send out *more* people to intercept Him. How come?

Centurion: I didn't want Him to trouble Himself, nor did I deserve to have Jesus come under my roof.

Reporter: You are in command of nearly one hundred men. Given your position and authority, you must realize how curiously backward that sounds.

Centurion: My authority is nothing compared to His. I have command over a few soldiers; He has command over nature and disease. If I can give an order and it gets followed regardless of my proximity to the soldier, certainly He can command sickness to leave the body from wherever He chooses.

Reporter: You make it sound as if that's painfully obvious, as if no proof or demonstration were required.

Centurion: Jesus has more than proven Himself. I'm amazed that so many of the "experts" refuse to believe Him.

Reporter: You raise a good point. Do you think Jesus was more amazed by your faith or their lack of it?

Centurion: I respect the Jewish people and am intrigued by their God. Notwithstanding, aspiring to behavioral perfection strikes me as fruitless and fairly vain. Perhaps in that regard, I had an advantage. I already knew I missed the mark. My *only* recourse was to humble myself and plead for Jesus' help.

Reporter: And you believe that's why Jesus healed your servant?

Centurion: I'm honored that He was amazed by my faith, but Jesus healed my servant because of who He is.

PRAYER FOCUS

Thank God for responding when we call on Him for help. Ask Him for the kind of faith that is amazing. Praise Him for His unmatched authority and compassion.

MOVING FORWARD

o   When you are desperate for help, is calling for Jesus your first response?

o   How does your faith compare to that of the centurion? Do you have the kind of faith that amazes Jesus? Explain.

o   Describe a time when Jesus showed up after you humbled yourself and asked.

The Ask Series

Some verses in the Bible are harder to understand than others, especially the ones about asking God for stuff. For your sake and our own, we wrestled and prayed and even cried our way through this next section, which is why the following pages might feel wonky—we're bringing some of our own heartbreak and confusion to bear in an effort to (1) understand, (2) accept, and (3) embrace what Jesus taught the disciples about asking.

Amanda wrote the first two.

Kristen wrote the second two.

Dallas helped.

But we're all in this together.

Buckle up. Theological rough road ahead.

ASK, GET HIM

"Ask, and it will be given to you; seek, and you will find; knock, and [the door] will be opened to you. For everyone who asks receives, and the one who seek finds, and to the one who knocks it will be opened. Or which one of you, if his son asks him for bread, will give him a stone? Or if he asks for a fish, will give him a serpent? If you then, who are evil, know how to give good gifts to your children, how much more will your Father who is in heaven give good things to those who ask him!"

MATTHEW 7:7–11

I really struggle with this passage. Because, come on. We simply don't always get what we ask God for. As I sit here typing, I'm waiting on my twelfth appliance repairman in less than twelve months. Both cars have been to the shop numerous times in those same twelve months, and both currently need to go back. The kids have been to the emergency room numerous times this year, and the bills are past due. Dallas and I have a kid in college, three more following close behind, and pretty much no ability to save a dime (see the previous moaning) let alone pay off the credit card bills. And of course, money-stress doesn't compare to the two new, serious health diagnoses for our children we're trying to navigate our way through.

But ask, and it will be given.

Hm.

Well I assure you, I've asked. Don't get me wrong. I'm aware of the ridiculousness of my whining, especially when I compare my woes to the people of first century AD. And of course, I don't even have to go back that far because there are plenty of people dealing with far greater trials than mine right here in the twenty-first century. But that doesn't change the fact that I don't like this passage because I don't totally understand it. And so I avoid it.

There's an interesting flow to the topics Jesus covers in Matthew 5–7, and they culminate in this very difficult-to-understand, very easy-to-misunderstand exhortation that begins with *ask, and it will be given.*

For the sake of clarity and context, Jesus compares God's way of giving to the way good parents give to their children. No stones or serpents in place of food—good parents provide for their kids. Good parents respond to their children's needs in love, action, wisdom, and grace.

It's also of note that good parents don't give serpents even when kids ask for them—and sometimes kids ask for them. Like children, we often want things that aren't good for us. It's the job of loving, engaged parents to say "no" or "not yet," as often as they say "yes" because we've all seen the social media posts, news segments, and daytime talk shows displaying the consequences of parents saying yes too often. Which means it's fair to say that our loving, all-wise, all-knowing heavenly Father doesn't and shouldn't say yes to everything we ask.

And yet, the ask and receive statement remains, so what the heck does it mean?

The answer becomes clearer in the verses that follow it. "Enter by the narrow gate. For the gate is wide and the way is easy that leads to destruction, and those who enter by it are many. For the gate is narrow and the way is hard that leads to life, and those who find it are few" (Matthew 7:13–14).

Clearly, the intention of the ask doctrine is not about having an ask-for-anything-you-want-and-you'll-get-it life, or Jesus wouldn't have followed it immediately with talk about how difficult it can be to follow Him. *The road is narrow. The way is hard.* The way wouldn't be hard if we could ask for and receive anything we wanted. Furthermore, when we read it again, it becomes clear that ask, seek, and knock are all referring to the same thing.

In context, when we ask, seek, and knock, we get God. He's the "it" of "ask, and *it* will be given." He's the One we find when we seek. He's the One who opens the door when we knock. We get Him. His goodness. His perspective. His intervention. His stamina. His wisdom. His patience. His steadfastness. His comfort. When He's the focus of our ask, He withholds nothing. We receive *who* we ask for.

Travelers on the wide road aren't required to surrender their will. They seek their own thing, pursue their own desires. On the narrow road (mapped out in Matthew 5–7), we follow

Jesus, which means we're not in control—we surrender our will, seek God's thing, pursue His desires, which are hard. And hard things are allowed by God so that we'll continually ask.

Perhaps instead of praying for my washing machine to miraculously start working, I'll ask God for His presence and peace of mind instead. Perhaps I'll ask that my difficult circumstances cause me to see Jesus more clearly. Perhaps I'll ask for resolve to use even my worst days for God's purposes.

Betcha I get a yes.

PRAYER FOCUS

Ask God to help you focus on spiritual growth as a solution to earthly struggles. Ask for the grace to see any hardship as an opportunity to ask, seek, and knock anew.

MOVING FORWARD

o   What are some of the challenging circumstances you're facing?

o   What does Matthew 7:7–11 reveal about God's heart, and how does that revelation change the way you view hard things?

o Write down a list of God's attributes that correlate with your circumstances, and ask Him to bring His resources and character to bear on whatever you're dealing with. (For example: Are you fearful? God is powerful, omniscient, and always available. Are you confused? God is wise, sovereign, and faithful.)

ASK, TRUST HIM

[Jesus] said to them… "Truly, I say to you, if you have faith like a grain of mustard seed, you will say to this mountain, 'Move from here to there,' and it will move, and nothing will be impossible for you."

MATTHEW 17:20

"Whatever you ask in my name, this I will do, that the Father may be glorified in the Son. If you ask me anything in my name, I will do it."

JOHN 14:13–14

This is the confidence that we have toward him, that if we ask anything according to his will he hears us. And if we know that he hears us in whatever we ask, we know that we have the requests that we have asked of him.

1 JOHN 5:14–15

Well, crud.

While it may be true that ask-seek-and-knock are contextually linked, there are plenty of other verses where the ask part goes rogue. And I suppose that's a good thing because while I'm learning to pray for more of God in the midst of financial woe (*Lord, please provide. Lord, use my lack to help me trust you more. Lord, free me from my love of money.*), I'm finding it way more difficult to pray that way when it comes to the people I love—especially since we're dealing with a few new medical diagnoses for our children that are (1) lifelong and (2) life-altering. My heart longs to pray for healing, so anything less would be insincere restraint. Still, when I see verses about having enough faith to move mountains, *we need only ask and believe*, my praying tongue gets tied.

And I have a really good reason.

One of our kids was diagnosed with autism at the age of three. Because she was non-verbal and had her own way of communicating, an acquaintance noticed our unique interaction at a birthday party and began asking questions. After a brief conversation, she told me that my daughter was autistic because I hadn't asked in faith for healing.

Oh.

My.

Gosh.

You may be surprised to hear I didn't punch her in the face. Truth is, I was more amused by the woman's total lack of social grace than I was hurt. For goodness sake, autism isn't a disease, and autistic people add a unique beauty to the world. Understatement. That said, autism does make life more challenging, and when we received our daughter's diagnosis, I grieved the struggles she would face. But it still didn't occur to me to ask God to remove it. She was *fearfully and wonderfully made* (Psalm 139:14)—and asking big was not my I-was-raised-a-Baptist way.

But the following morning, God pressed on my heart to ask. Just ask. With all the child-like faith I could muster, I prayed my bravest, boldest prayer: that God would put words in my baby's mouth. When I went to her room, I was hopeful her tongue would be loosed. I really was. I had overlooked an offense and responded to the Holy Spirit's prompting to step out in faith. I had asked for a mountain to be moved and believed in God's power to move it. All the boxes were checked.

And then God didn't move the mountain.

It felt like a setup. I'd made myself vulnerable to hope only to be left standing on an ill-advised ledge—and I've been praying general prayers for *God's kingdom come, His will be done* ever since because I got burned when I got specific. But the verses inviting us to get specific remain, so I suppose it's time to try to understand them.

As always, context matters. In fact, context is a saving grace when we're confused by something God has said or done or allowed. In the days that followed my prayer-fail, I found my footing in God's character. He is good, He is kind, He is love—those were the things I knew to be true in spite of my disappointment and confusion. I clung to what I knew.

Scripture context matters too, which is why most of us don't own a mansion. God bless John because he provides the context and the key ingredient to moving mountains: we ask *according to God's will.* In other words, God is not subject to our mountain-moving whims. And simply put, my desire to see my child's brain work differently was not God's desire—it wasn't His will for her life. So why did God press on my heart to ask Him for something He wasn't going to give?

To practice asking.

And maybe that sounds mean—at least, that's what I used to think, but I don't anymore. God is the Creator and Healer, Redeemer and Restorer—and more often than not, we don't act like we actually believe it. We don't act like we have access to the One who throws mountains into the sea, and so we forgo opportunities to sit in a front row seat when He does. Asking puts us in a front row seat.

Thing is, I don't know God's will. I know His commands. I know His heart. I know the Bible; I'm growing in my understanding of it more and more as the years go by, and so my prayers more often reflect His priorities and will. But I still don't *know* God's will in regard to the intricacies of life. I don't know why He allows hard things or why He chooses to sometimes remove hard things. But I do know that God knows all the things I don't—He knows everything. So I ask in faith because He can do anything. And then I can trust Him regardless of His answer because in His sovereign wisdom and abounding love, God will do everything that aligns with His perfect will.

And I wanna be there when He does.

PRAYER FOCUS

Ask God to help you wrestle through the profoundly difficult aspects of asking. Ask Him to help you rest in His will. And ask Him to loose your tongue to pray big prayers.

MOVING FORWARD

o   What experiences have caused you to feel disappointed by God?

o   What aspects of God's character can you cling to while you wait for understanding?

o   What are you asking God for? Ask Him with boldness and faith because of His ability to do the impossible. And then also ask that He will increase your ability to trust Him with the answers to your asks.

ASK WHATEVER OF HIM

"I tell you, whatever you ask for in prayer, believe that you have received it, and it will be yours."

MARK 11:24

Asking for whatever sounds simple enough but waxes more complicated when put into practice. The asking part is pretty straightforward. We know how to want stuff. It's the receiving bit where the wheels can fall off. You know, because we don't always get what we asked for.

Since we don't know God's will, and feeling like unanswered spiritual losers is the opposite of what we're going for, not asking seems like the better, safer option. Sure, we'll never get the whatever, but at least we won't have to deal with all that pesky discouragement.

Fortunately, Jesus does not share the aforementioned sentiment, and He tells us repeatedly to ask for whatever.

Why? Because what we want matters to God. He baked many of those wants directly into our DNA, and there are certain whatevers He's eager to answer for the sake of His kingdom and glory. Incidentally, the same could be said of our deficiencies—they, too, matter, and God wants to use them (more on that later).

As it turns out, God knows everything about the difficult situation you're in. He knows exactly how it should be resolved and where your weak, inadequate self fits into the equation. It's because of this that He invites you to ask for whatever. This isn't a new concept. God woke Solomon up in the middle of the night to extend the same offer. Solomon wasn't wise yet, but he was smart enough to take God up on it.

Shortly after, Solomon was appointed king by his father David:

> The Lord appeared to Solomon during the night in a dream, and God said, "Ask for whatever you want me to give you." Solomon answered,… "Now, Lord my God, you have made your servant king in place of my father David. But I am only a child and do not know how to carry out my duties…. So give your servant a discerning heart to govern your people and to distinguish between right and wrong." (1 Kings 3:5–6, 7, 9 NIV)

God was pleased with Solomon's whatever and honored his ask. Then He blessed him a silly amount extra just for fun, making Solomon the wisest and richest man who ever lived.

Why? Because God knew the situation: Solomon was a new king. God knew the deficiency: Solomon was a clueless new king. God knew the want: Solomon was a clueless new king who wanted to govern well.

It's the same with us. He invites us to ask for whatever so He can meet the need, resolve the situation, and reveal His will in the process. We're only spiritual losers when we foolishly decline the miraculous offer. Safer is never better when it comes to prayer.

And if you don't happen to receive the whatever, then ask God to search your heart and show you why. Maybe it's a timing thing. Or maybe it's not for you. Whatever the reason, don't get discouraged. If your main whatever is to glorify God and build His kingdom, He'll be pleased with your ask and will most certainly honor it. And who knows, you may even get the silly amount extra.

PRAYER FOCUS

Thank God that what we want actually matters to Him. Ask for something big enough that failure is guaranteed unless He shows up. Praise Him for being mighty enough to do it!

MOVING FORWARD

o   Do you sometimes feel like it's a better, safer option to not ask God for *whatever*? Why or why not?

o   God knows the situation, the deficiency, and the need. What might He be inviting you to ask for right now?

o Our main *whatever* should always be to glorify God and build His kingdom. Start by asking for that and record how He answers you.

ASK, GET THE BEST FROM HIM

Three times I pleaded with the Lord to take it away from me. But he said to me, "My grace is sufficient for you, for my power is made perfect in weakness." Therefore I will boast all the more gladly about my weaknesses, so that Christ's power may rest on me.

2 Corinthians 12:8–9 NIV

It's true. Solomon got his *whatever*. God more than compensated for his deficiency. It's also true that the apostle Paul did not get his. He asked God to remove the "thorn in his flesh," but it never happened.

That thorn Paul referred to in 2 Corinthians 12:7 will forever be a mystery. Theologians and others have speculated upon it for centuries, surmising that Paul suffered with everything from a gnarly eye disease to PTSD to malaria to same-sex attraction. Whatever the case, it was chronic, debilitating, and felt life-ruining enough to bring tough-guy Paul to his knees. Three times he pleaded with the Lord to take it away.

God, on the other hand, preferred what the thorn produced in Paul, and He kept it right where it was. Compared to Solomon, it seems as though Paul got the short end of the "ask *whatever*" stick. But he didn't. Paul asked for relief, and God gave it to him. He just did it with the thorn still firmly wedged in his aching flesh.

We all have thorns; not one of us is exempt. And every thorn, be it big or small, is purposeful. One of my chronic, debilitating thorns is still firmly wedged in my brain. I am dyslexic and have a sequencing disorder, which makes recalling and assimilating information extremely challenging at times. My comprehension gets jumbled or completely stuck like a soda bottle in a vending machine. It's seemingly within reach but snagged on something internal, unable to make its way out. I can't help but want to shake and kick the machine.

More often than not, my brain charitably decides to function normally. Still, everything I do makes for a guessing game. For example, if I were to read out loud, one of two things would happen: I'd either breeze through it effortlessly or just stare at the nonsensical word mess like a confused monkey. It's so fun, this game, and not at all embarrassing.

Truth be told, it's been a painful thorn, especially when I was young. The insecurity it bred was devastating. School was an absolute nightmare, and I felt like the dumbest kid ever. It's been a few years, so yes—I've recovered from the emotional trauma that was high school and managed to do well in college and beyond. But I still feel weak. It's been a big *whatever* in my life, and I've pleaded with the Lord countless times to take it away. Thus far He has chosen not to. Evidently He prefers what it produces in my life, which is humility, intimacy, and dependence on Him.

So here's the thing: God answered Paul every bit as much as He answered Solomon, and He's answered me every bit as much as He answered Paul. He has more than compensated for *all* our deficiencies. Whether we're clueless and need wisdom or hurting and need relief, His grace is sufficient, and His power is made perfect in weakness.

Through my thorn, I've come to understand exactly that—with crystal clear comprehension, by the way. God's grace, which He has more than lavished on me, is not a consolation prize; it's the ultimate prize. It's more of Jesus because it's His strength working in and through me. Therefore I, Kristen Hendricks, will boast all the more gladly about my dyslexic brain so that Christ's power may rest on me.

PRAYER FOCUS

Thank God that His strength is made perfect in your weakness. Ask Him to reveal how each and every thorn in your life can glorify Him. Praise Him for compensating for all of your deficiencies.

MOVING FORWARD

o What thorn(s) have you repeatedly asked God to remove and why?

o What has been your attitude toward God when it comes to your thorn? Does your perspective regarding its presence and purpose in your life need to change?

o How has His grace strengthened you and proven to be sufficient?

EXPECTATIONS

> When John heard in prison about the deeds of the Christ, he
> sent word by his disciples and said to him, "Are you the one
> who is to come, or shall we look for another?"
>
> MATTHEW 11:2–3

What a raw and revealing question from one of Christianity's top dogs.

John the Baptizer had been proclaiming the coming Messiah—it was the God-given purpose of his miraculously conceived life (Luke 1:5–13). He preached with complete abandon, spreading his "repent and be ready" message in spite of all the social and religious alienation that came with it. He was all in. He lived off the land (ate bugs), wore it on his back (camel hair), and Bible-banged (preached real loud) to anyone who would listen. And then he actually baptized Jesus and witnessed "the heavens [opening], and he saw the Spirit of God descending like a dove and coming to rest on [Jesus]; and behold, a voice from heaven said, 'This is my beloved Son, with whom I am well pleased'" (Matthew 3:16–17).

One can only imagine what the voice from heaven sounded like. No doubt experiencing it was a confirmation of John's already humungo faith that the Messiah was coming and was already here.

As if that weren't enough, then came the miracles. Jesus was gathering followers and moving from town to town, preaching and healing and astonishing the crowds. And all the while John was doing his thing, calling for repentance and pointing people to Jesus. "'I am not the Christ, but I have been sent before him.' … Therefore this joy of mine is now complete. [Jesus] must increase, but I must decrease" (John 3:28–30).

John was faith-filled.

Until he landed in prison.

John quickly discovered that unmet expectations can be totally derailing. Underneath his truly impressive and genuine faith, there was still the capacity to question and doubt. He wasn't immune from fear or frustration. And in this jail cell moment, it's possible he even felt abandoned and betrayed by the One he'd devoted his life to. For crying out loud, from all accounts it appears that Jesus didn't even visit His faithful servant-cousin in prison.

But remember, John had really good reasons for having a strong faith. He had witnessed miraculous things and had even been written into the story—for grief's sake, he was a fulfillment of prophecy, the forerunner of the long-awaited Messiah (Isaiah 40:3). But in spite of all he knew, he wavered because humanity's MO is to question and doubt when things go badly. We just do. And God's MO in those moments is to remind us of who He is, in spite of how things appear.

"Jesus answered them, 'Go and tell John what you hear and see: the blind receive their sight and the lame walk, lepers are cleansed and the deaf hear, and the dead are raised up, and the poor have good news preached to them. And blessed is the one who is not offended by me'" (Matthew 11:4–6).

Jesus' response to John was simple: remember what you know about me. In other words, *Don't let this moment derail you, my good and faithful servant. I AM who I say I AM, even when your expectations go unmet.*

Jesus wasn't upset with John. He wasn't incredulous that John was having a moment—quite the opposite. He turned back to the crowd and publicly honored John's big dog faith (v. 11), because Jesus is patient and kind, and He knows that unmet expectations can be really hard. That said, He's also not held hostage by our doubt or disappointment, as though He has to prove Himself—He's already done that.

Jesus didn't go visit John in prison, and He didn't get Him out. And then John was executed. But the moment after he lost his life, John was raised to life in heaven, where his faith became sight and his ears heard the words, *Well done, my good and faithful servant.*

And all the earthly expectations he ever had were far surpassed.

PRAYER FOCUS

Thank God for longsuffering with you in your doubt and disappointment and ask Him to increase your faithfulness. Thank Him for who He is and for being worthy of your trust.

MOVING FORWARD

o What expectations in your life have gone unmet, and how have you handled your disappointment?

o Read Psalm 42:11, Isaiah 40:28–31, and Romans 8:28. How do these verses impact the way you process hard things?

o Do you believe God is who He says He is? Meaning... do you reeeeeally believe that He's always good and kind and wise and just? Be honest—with yourself and with Him—because most of us don't *always* believe *all* those things *all* the time.

FAITH KILLER

When Herod heard John, he was greatly puzzled;
yet he liked to listen to him.

MARK 6:20 NIV

Herod Antipas is not a super relatable guy. The story of a Roman tetrarch who marries his brother's wife and offers her daughter anything she wants after entertaining a room full of military commanders with an R-rated dance is not a person most of us identify with. And that's a good thing, especially since it culminates with her requesting John the Baptist's head on a platter and Herod complying. So—we really hope you don't relate to that.

For all the same reasons, Herod Antipas is not a super likeable guy. Not only was he responsible for the death of John the Baptist, he (spoiler alert) had a small part in the execution of Jesus as well. But prior to all the murdering, there was a glimmer of hope. There was just enough softness in Herod's heart to draw him toward John's preaching. So what happened? Where did it all go terribly wrong? Simply put, Herod was worried about looking bad and would have done anything to preserve his reputation.

Before the beheading, Herod imprisoned John because he publicly rebuked him for his adulterous marriage. It wasn't just creepy that the king stole his brother's wife; it was illegal. Once the people caught wind of Herod's scandalous marriage situation, they were outraged. It was a public relations nightmare and bad for business. So at his wife's prompting, Herod locked John up to shut John up.

Despite the personal reproof, Herod still enjoyed listening to what John had to say. After being surrounded by a slew of yes-men and self-interested parasites, he likely appreciated John's candor. If John was willing to publicly rebuke Herod for his sinful marriage, surely he privately exhorted him to repent and believe. That was John's life's work, after all. What's amazing is that Herod actually listened. He was puzzled by it, but he listened.

Unfortunately, he listened to others more. In front of a room full of important people, after being prompted by her vengeful mother, the dancing girl asked Herod for John's head. Even though he was greatly distressed by the perverse demand, Herod folded like a lawn chair and ordered the executioner to get on with it.

And that was that. Once again, Herod made the epically stupid decision to protect his power by grasping at the ever-shifting approval of man. He cared more about saving face than saving John, hence impulsively murdering the greatest man ever born of a woman (Matthew 11:11).

Although we can't relate to Herod's bio, we can relate to his predicament. Fear of man, a.k.a. people pleasing, is a soul-crushing faith killer. It may not lead to murder, but it will always strangle spiritual growth.

Imagine what might've happened if Herod had said, "Good grief, girl, what's the matter with you? Ask for something normal like a pony." But he didn't. Sadly, in his twisted quest to be loved by his wicked wife, accepted by the masses, and esteemed by his colleagues, Herod Antipas became one of the most despised men in all of history.

How's that for ironic?

PRAYER FOCUS

Ask the Lord to reveal where people pleasing affects your life the most. Pray for help in finding your favor in God, not man. Praise God that you don't have to save face with Him.

MOVING FORWARD

o You may not consider yourself a people pleaser, but fear of man or desiring the approval of others affects everyone. How does it play out in your social life, work life, and family life?

o Recall an instance when you folded to peer pressure or for the sake of preserving your reputation. How would the outcome have changed had you responded biblically?

o   Based on 1 Samuel 16:7, we can see that all the street cred in the world doesn't impress God. What is God most concerned with, and how would your life be different if you cared more about His priorities than anyone else's?

DEVOTED

He went up on the mountain and called to him
those whom he desired, and they came to him. And he
appointed twelve (whom he also named apostles) so that
they might be with him and he might send them out to
preach and have authority to cast out demons.

MARK 3:13–15

"I want you, you, you, you, you, you, you, you, you, you, you, and you."

That was the day Jesus recruited the rest of His disciples. He picked the team that would impact the world more than any other group of men in the history of mankind. Judas was in that group. Which means that per His Father's instruction, Jesus handpicked the man who would betray Him with a kiss. Of course, Judas didn't know that. He couldn't foresee his impending downfall. He had no clue what his greed would set in motion and how it would ultimately lead to both of their deaths. That day, Judas was likely thrilled. Out of a mountainside full of people, he was picked for Jesus' elite traveling team.

We don't know anything about the exchange other than it happened. Why did Judas willingly give up everything and go with Jesus? Was he momentarily sincere in his seeking, or was he a power-loving opportunist looking to exploit the people amazed by Jesus? We don't know (but we explore it in *The Chosen*).

But we do know this: he could've changed. Judas wasn't locked in to being Judas. He was afforded every opportunity to kick his greedy habits and grow in faithfulness and obedience. His experience was no different from that of the other disciples. Jesus taught Judas. He sent Judas out to preach. Presumably, Judas even received authority to drive out demons. Nowhere does it say: *The eleven legit disciples were sent out while the bogus disciple, Judas, hung back at camp.* As far as we know, Judas was learning and doing all the things that the disciples were chosen and appointed to do. He just did them with a rotten heart.

Judas was a self-serving, greedy thief, which is a rough weakness to have when you've committed to following a homeless preacher. But so was Matthew, remember, and since he was a wealthy tax collector, he likely had a heck of a lot more to lose. Yet the shift from excessively rich to sleeping-on-the-ground poor didn't faze Matthew. How come? Because Matthew was devoted to Jesus. Judas was not.

Judas was the poster boy for Matthew 6:24. "No one can serve two masters, for either he will hate the one and love the other, or he will be devoted to the one and despise the other. You cannot serve both God and money."

Obviously Judas was devoted to the money. What's mind-bendingly beautiful is that Jesus still served Judas because Jesus was devoted to His Father. He obeyed His Father's instruction and submitted to His will, even when it came to His own betrayer. He knew that despite Judas's opportunity to change, he never would. Judas would remain a self-serving, greedy thief throughout the three-year-long process. But more importantly, Jesus knew that His Father would never change. He'd still be the sovereign God of the universe guiding His every selfless move.

It must've made recruiting His betrayer a lot easier that day. Because it was never about whether Judas would be obedient and stay the course.

It was proof that Jesus would.

PRAYER FOCUS

Thank God for Jesus' willingness to submit to His Father's will. Ask Him to reveal anything you're more devoted to than Him. Praise Him for being worthy of loyalty.

MOVING FORWARD

o What aspects of Jesus' character does His relationship with Judas cause you to ponder and why?

o   Since we are to be Christ-like, how might His example apply to you? Who are you called to serve out of obedience to the Father?

o   Read through Matthew 6:19–24. What in this passage convicts you?

GET THE PRIZE

"Not everyone who says to me, 'Lord, Lord,'
will enter the kingdom of heaven, but only the one
who does the will of my Father who is in heaven."

MATTHEW 7:21

Judas was picked for the team, but he never got the prize. He betrayed Jesus. We all know that. But how could he? Why did he? And what does that mean for us?

Writing one devotional entry about Judas is hard enough, much less two. But the sobering implications of his relationship with Jesus are difficult to move through quickly. This guy was physically with Jesus for three whole years…think about that. He saw the miracles. He heard the preaching. Judas witnessed Jesus' compassion, character, and humility. He watched Him pray. What was wrong with this disciple that resulted in such a hateful response to the incarnation of perfect love?

Typically, Judas is portrayed as some ridiculous archetype villain. Vaudeville Judas would have had the slick handlebar mustache and a black cloak. He'd snicker and rub his hands together while plotting dastardly deeds. But that's just dumb. Truth is, Judas was deceptively normal. He fit right in with the rest of the fellas, and they were as shocked as anyone to learn he was the betrayer. Had he been archetype villain Judas, everyone would've responded, "Obviously! We saw that coming."

It wasn't obvious. Maybe not even to Judas. We don't know. Clearly he was tempted, and of course, he absolutely and premeditatedly blew it. But so did David. David committed adultery then concocted a dastardly plot of his own to kill Bathsheba's husband (2 Samuel 11). Yet we still know him as the "man after God's own heart" (Acts 13:22). Aaron was still allowed to be the high priest after caving to peer pressure and crafting an idol for the Israelites to worship and dance naked around (Exodus 32). Judas didn't know about Peter's threefold denial situation (Luke 22:54–62), but if he did, I bet he'd argue it was just as bad as the offense he committed, if not worse.

Needless to say, throughout Scripture there are tons of egregious, shameful, butt-saving, stupid mistakes committed by messed up people who were failing forward as they tried to follow the Lord. So why was Judas the one classified as "doomed to destruction" (John 17:12 NIV)? Why was his mistake so much worse? Because he wasn't failing forward; he was just failing. He may've been doing disciple things, but he wasn't trying to follow the Lord.

He wasn't devoted to Jesus because he refused to know Jesus.

As it turns out, going through the motions of ministry and surrendering your heart and life to Christ are two very different things. Judas called Jesus, "Lord." He did all the churchy, disciple activities, and probably even did some miracles like the rest of them, but he failed to do the will of the Father in heaven, which is to know His Son *personally*.

The most sobering part is that Judas is in good company. "Many will say to me on that day, 'Lord, Lord, did we not prophesy in your name and in your name drive out demons and in your name perform many miracles?' Then I will tell them plainly, 'I never knew you. Away from me you evildoers!'" (Matthew 7:22–23 NIV).

Many will say.

Many.

Not just the betrayer, Judas.

There are many deceptively normal people going through the churchy motions who don't know Jesus personally. That's so scary, but I suppose it should be. What could be more terrifying than Jesus saying, "I never knew you"?

The answer? *Nothing*. Nothing at all, so make sure that He does know you.

If you haven't surrendered your life to Jesus, make this your moment. Right now. He has already chosen you. Choose Him back. Respond appropriately to His perfect love and get the prize.

PRAYER FOCUS

Thank God that He has already picked you for His team. Tell Him you want to know Him even better. Praise Him for the opportunity to know Him personally.

MOVING FORWARD

o If you haven't fully trusted Jesus with your life, pray something like this:

Father, I've gone my own way and sinned against you. Have mercy on me and forgive my sin. I believe in your Son, who died in my place then rose from the dead with the power and authority to give me a new life. Thank you for making me a child of God. I now surrender my life to you and your purposes. Give me by your Holy Spirit the boldness to confess my faith in you to others and to keep following you all the days of my life. I ask this in your Son's name, Jesus. Amen.

THE HOUSE
THAT STANDS

"Why do you call me 'Lord, Lord,'
and not do what I tell you?"

LUKE 6:46

The people following Jesus around had a lord problem. They didn't have an attendance problem; they showed up to hear Him preach. Or a curiosity problem; they stayed and watched and listened. Or a positive-feelings-toward-Jesus problem; they, no doubt, really liked the miraculous things He was doing. By all accounts, His words and His way were fascinating and crowd-drawing. But the people had a lord problem, and it didn't take long for Jesus to call them out.

Truth be told, most of us don't like being under authority. Respecting the lordship of another requires deference and humility, even obedience. And in our me-first, happiness-above-all, truth-is-relative-so-make-your-own-way world, the concept of relinquishing our right to choose anything can be downright offensive. Lordship removes our right to choose what we think is best for ourselves.

And nothing is new under the sun because the people hanging around Jesus had similar issues in spite of their wildly different circumstances. They were actually under the heavy-handed and cruel authority of Rome, and they were sick of it. They were submitting and suffering and, no doubt, understandably equating the two.

Then along came a man who was super interesting and did cool things, but calling Him Lord? Um, no thanks, Jesus. We'd rather just take in the show and be on our way.

Humans, no matter the situation, prefer to not bend the knee.

And yet Jesus made a case for doing just that.

"Everyone who comes to me and hears my words and does them…is like a man building a house, who dug deep and laid the foundation on the rock. And when the flood arose, the stream broke against that house and could not shake it, because it had been well built. But the one who hears and does not do them is like a man who built a house on the ground without a foundation. When the stream broke against it, immediately it fell, and the ruin of it was great" (Luke 6:47–49).

Jesus was not a teacher of take-it-or-leave-it things. And He wasn't healing so that people's lives would be easier. He healed to prove His lordship and, yes, because He's a kind and compassionate Lord. But He didn't promise that following Him would result in flood prevention—as the parable goes, the man built his house on the rock so that *when* the flood came, it wasn't able to destroy the house. And Jesus is the Rock, the sure foundation we can trust. He's worthy of our digging deep and bowing low because our life will be preserved if we do the things He says. If we defer to His authority and call Him Lord.

Conversely (and far more commonly), the man who did his own thing, trusting in his own wisdom, lost everything. He may have felt good about his house while it stood, but without the one sure foundation, it ultimately came to ruin; as will our self-centered, self-directed lives if we make the same mistake. Calling Jesus "Lord" means recognizing the authority He already has. He made the world and everything in it, so people should do the things He says, because—duh. As the little girl in Episode 3, Season 1 of *The Chosen* says, "He's smart, so we should listen!"

But far more often, people trust in themselves and cling to a false sense of control. Like the crowds in Jesus' day, far too many show up at church and celebrate the Jesus holidays while fundamentally and foundationally refusing His authority.

And great will be their fall.

PRAYER FOCUS

Ask God to show you where you've refused His authority and done your own thing. Ask for forgiveness and pray for strength to relinquish your will and replace it with His. And if you've never actually called Jesus "Lord," change that today— because it's never too late to bend the knee.

MOVING FORWARD

o   Is Jesus your Lord? Why or why not?

o   What does the word "submission" conjure in your mind and heart?

o   Read Exodus 34:6, Deuteronomy 32:4, and Psalm 145:8. How does the concept of submission change when you're reminded that the One you are submitting to is all of these things and more?

SELL OUT

Jesus looked at him and loved him. "One thing you lack," he said. "Go, sell everything you have and give to the poor, and you will have treasure in heaven. Then come, follow me." At this the man's face fell. He went away sad, because he had great wealth.

MARK 10:21–22 NIV

Rich people can go to heaven. It's just not super easy for them because convincing a wealthy person to give up their luxury import and walk through the narrow gate with a bunch of poor people is a tough sell. Why be uncomfortable if you can drive through your own wider, fancier gate with a top-of-the-line security system?

Let's be real. Regardless of the tax bracket we're in, our natural inclination is to clench our greedy mitts around anything that can protect us from desperation, neediness, and want. Money seems to be the most obvious thing to grasp. So who is willing to give it all up once they have it? Answer:

hardly anyone. In fact, it's such a miniscule fraction of the population that Jesus used hyperbole to emphasize the point: "It is easier for a camel to go through the eye of a needle than for someone who is rich to enter the kingdom of God" (Mark 10:25 NIV). That's sad because there are a lot of rich people. Parenthetically, if you have a home, running water, refrigeration, and the means to purchase this devotional book, "rich" includes you.

The rich guy in Mark chapter 10 knows how devastatingly sad it really is. He started out with good intentions. He was so eager to talk to Jesus that he literally ran to meet Him. Once there, he was humble and deferential. He bowed. Zealous in his query, he needed to know what he must do to inherit eternal life. This is not the behavior of a rich Pharisee-type looking to justify himself. The question was earnest and personal.

Jesus first responded by listing commandments 6, 7, 8, 9, and 5. The big ones: Don't murder, don't commit adultery, don't steal, don't give false testimony, and honor your parents. Although the rich guy had been keeping those commandments since he was a boy, Jesus knew his heart and his Achilles heel.

Jesus looked at him and loved him, told him to go sell all his stuff and give the money to the poor, then come back and follow Him. That's a big ask no matter how you slice it, but that's what love does: it calls out our sin and orders our steps so we can become desperate and needy for Him.

But the rich guy couldn't do it. He couldn't unclench his materialistic mitts and let Jesus rescue him from the bondage of earthly wealth. After keeping all those commandments for all those years, he failed to obey the first and biggest one: *You shall have no other gods before me.*

The revelation must have gutted him. The rich guy locked eyes with the Messiah, felt His love, grasped that money was no longer the most obvious thing…and yet still chose to worship his inferior god. Describing the man as "sad" seems like a profound understatement since the poor guy walked away with his wealth intact but also the worst imaginable poverty.

He didn't have Jesus.

PRAYER FOCUS

Ask the Lord to search your heart for idols. Trust Him with the blessings He allows you to steward as well as the ones He asks you to give up. Praise Him for providing all of your needs, all the time.

MOVING FORWARD

o   You don't have to be financially well off to relate to this guy. In what ways do you believe money can keep you from desperation, neediness, and want?

o   Jesus knows your heart and your Achilles heel, whether it's money or something else. What would He ask you to give up to focus more on Him?

o   Read Philippians 4:12–13. How would life be different if you, like the apostle Paul, learned the secret of true contentment?

FOLLOW LIKE

Soon afterward he went on through cities and villages, proclaiming and bringing the good news of the kingdom of God. And the twelve were with him, and also some women who had been healed of evil spirits and infirmities: Mary, called Magdalene, from whom seven demons had gone out, and Joanna, the wife of Chuza, Herod's household manager, and Susanna, and many others, who provided for them out of their means.

LUKE 8:1–3

Women weren't treated well in Jesus' day. Understatement. They had few choices, held no positions, and were considered to be less valuable than the men.

But not to Jesus.

The adulterous woman was caught in the act and dragged to Jesus for judgment. But He called her accusers hypocrites, dispersed the crowd, and extended her grace (John 8:3–11). The bleeding woman found Jesus and, upon touching His robe, was immediately healed of her twelve-year-long affliction. In front of the crowd that had deemed her unclean, Jesus honored her for her faith (Luke 8:43–48). The Samaritan woman was drawing water from the community well at the hottest time of day. Translation: she was likely avoiding people because of her seedy reputation. But ahead of everyone else on earth, Jesus told *her* He was the Savior they'd been waiting for. And she got to tell the others (John 4:1–30).

Bottom line: when the world chose to abuse, alienate, and brutally judge these women, Jesus rescued, restored, and redeemed them. He ascribed them value because that's what He does.

So it's no wonder that Jesus' entourage included women. They'd been on the receiving end of His power and grace, their bodies and hearts healed and set free. They followed Him alongside the twelve and financially supported His three-year-long ministry—all the while listening, watching, and learning. And that's of note because while Jesus affirmed women's God-given value, He still called twelve men to be His apostles. Only men.

Gulp.

Gender isn't an awesome topic for a devotional. That is, unless talking about it somehow points us all—male and female alike—back to Jesus. And that would be quite a trick since it's far more likely to leave us feeling defensive and confused. But it's also impossible to avoid sometimes, so instead of allowing it to derail our faith in Jesus or our relationships across the gender aisle, it's important to see ourselves the way our Creator does. And to defer to what the Creator does.

Three things are true.

- God created both men and women in His own image, and both are necessary to fully reflect His countless attributes. Individually, we just don't cut it (Genesis 1:27).

- God created every single human with loving intention and care, which includes our gender, and that means a) our gender matters to God and b) both genders matter to God (Psalm 139:13–14).

- Jesus called twelve men to be His apostles upon whom He built the early church. And then Paul got down to brass tacks and said things that make some women uncomfortable (that's a whole different book), but the truth is Jesus set the precedent for male leadership, not Paul (Luke 6:12–16).

Jesus called twelve men, that's just true. And He was surrounded by dedicated women whose lives had been fundamentally and radically changed by His rescue. Also true. The rest of us are supposed to follow in their footsteps because we've *all* been rescued. And since being lost without Jesus is the one thing all humans have in common regardless of gender, there's not a lot of room left for arrogance or defensiveness or bitterness over who does what.

Instead we should be overjoyed and eager to follow Jesus like the apostles did, like Mary of Magdala did, like Joanna and Susanna did because we, too, have been saved by the One who rescues, restores, and redeems. Jesus is the One who ascribes to us our value. *And* because He is good and kind and worthy of our trust, we can stop jockeying for position and rest in His love, focus on His work, and wait for heaven to understand why He assigned certain tasks to certain people.

PRAYER FOCUS

Thank God for the opportunity you have to follow Jesus. Thank Him for your brothers and sisters in the faith. Ask God to help you accept and understand the Bible even when it's hard. And ask that He'd help you rest in Jesus' love for you, His unique and precious creation.

MOVING FORWARD

o   What's your rescued-by-Jesus story?

o   In what ways have you been blessed by a brother in Christ? By a sister in Christ?

o   Satan would prefer us to focus on the things that divide because the church of Christ ceases to be effective when there's in-fighting. But Jesus says, "The last will be first, and the first last" (Matthew 20:16). What does that verse mean to you, and how would gender relations be impacted if we truly lived by it?

SENT

He called the twelve together and gave them power and authority over all demons and to cure diseases, and he sent them out to proclaim the kingdom of God and to heal. And he said to them, "Take nothing for your journey, no staff, nor bag, nor bread, nor money; and do not have two tunics. And whatever house you enter, stay there, and from there depart. And wherever they do not receive you, when you leave that town shake off the dust from your feet as a testimony against them."

LUKE 9:1–5

Those were pretty specific and also terrifying marching orders. The disciples were being sent into the countryside to do what they'd been watching Jesus do, without food or shelter. Or power. Jesus was asking them to trust His word that provision for all of the above would manifest when needed.

Of course, unlike road trips today, there weren't pit stops along the way. There weren't exits every few miles with options for snacks, bathrooms, and hotels. Heck, even with the ability to stop and refuel at will, we *still* pack snacks. But these guys were told to set out with nothing but the shirts on their backs. They couldn't even bring a staff, which they would've used as both a walking stick through tough terrain and a weapon of self-defense against wild animals and bad guys.

Boiled down, the plan was "take nothing because you'll be provided for in your moment of need." Despite the unknown and all the scary scenarios that came with it, they went as Jesus sent them. Just imagine the first day of that journey… the amount of faith they must've had in Jesus to take the initial steps. No supplies and no plan other than walking and preaching and healing, which none of them had ever even done before. It's remarkable they didn't all defect right then and there.

So why didn't they? We marvel at their faith, but like us, these guys were far from perfect. And they certainly weren't brave. They were scared of the Romans, they were intimidated by the Pharisees, they repeatedly became overwhelmed when crowds got too big or too needy, and they were terrified when a great big storm arose.

"And they went and woke him, saying, 'Master, Master, we are perishing!' And he awoke and rebuked the wind and the raging waves, and they ceased, and there was a calm. He said to them, 'Where is your faith?' And they were afraid, and they marveled, saying to one another, 'Who then is this, that he commands even winds and water, and they obey him?'" (Luke 8:24–25).

So what enabled twelve ordinary men to step out in

extraordinary faith? Well, it's not a coincidence that Jesus' directive when sending them came after many moments like the one on the lake, in which He proved Himself worthy of being obeyed. Simply put, these flawed men had experienced enough of Jesus to trust Him. They didn't necessarily feel ready—most of us never really do. But God knows when we've seen enough of His faithfulness, power, and presence to start taking bigger steps on the walk of faith.

As it turned out, the combination of take nothing/receive everything was a winning one. Because when we offer ourselves to Jesus, believing in faith that He'll be faithful, He enters into our lack, replacing it with more and more and more of Himself. For the disciples, that meant seeing people healed, body and soul, en masse.

But it started with being sent.

PRAYER FOCUS

Ask God to open your eyes to His constant presence along with all the ways He's been faithful to provide for your needs. Ask Him to grow your faith in His faithfulness and for the courage to go where He sends you.

MOVING FORWARD

o When it comes to following and obeying Jesus, what do you fear?

o The disciples shared many of our fears. Can you fear less now that you've seen how God met their needs?

o Read 2 Corinthians 4:7 and 2 Corinthians 12:9–10. Like the disciples, we're weak, imperfect, ordinary people. But according to these verses, why does that have zero bearing on how God uses us?

WATCH OUT

I am afraid that as the serpent deceived Eve by his cunning, your thoughts will be led astray by a sincere and pure devotion to Christ. For if someone comes and proclaims another Jesus than the one we proclaimed, or if you receive a different spirit from the one you received, or if you accept a different gospel from the one you accepted, you put up with it readily enough.

2 Corinthians 11:3–4

The Great Deceiver is one of Satan's most befitting monikers. He's the ultimate lying liar who lies and will stop at nothing to separate us from God. His tactics haven't evolved since the garden; he's just hyper-adept at staying ahead of the curve, especially within the church.

He's been the campaign manager for many post-modern religious movements, eagerly orchestrating all the moving parts. The Great Deceiver's specialty is branding, but he's more than happy to help with menial tasks such as float building and sign painting. Once the message has been embraced, the perfect influencers are dispatched to deliver the goods. They toss candy and false doctrine in equal measure.

The Great Deceiver is very interested in your feelings, opinions, and personal preferences. He's quite progressive that way and wants to hear *all* about it. Your concerns are His concerns. And he knows exactly which one-off rendition of Jesus is pertinent to your cause. As of late, it's likely to be a socially relevant, notably liberal Jesus who somehow cares more about your truth than the truth He came to personify, proclaim, and die for—but let's not get bogged down with details or definitions. We're graduating from all that antiquated stuff, remember?

How 'bout a new gospel, the *Twenty-first Century Western Sensibilities* edition? It doesn't matter whether it's a counterfeit gospel as long as we all remain true to ourselves. But, hold up! That last sentence is way too wordy. For the sake of effective branding, let's shorten it to: The gospel of your own truth. Yes. Better. That'll preach! Now just to be clear, no one is saying you have to give up your faith in Jesus, but obviously some of His outdated theology needs revamping because it no longer works today. A good chunk of it is offensive enough to be considered a hate crime, especially that bit about marriage and sexuality. Jesus told His followers to love one another, not judge one another. So who are you to judge how others love one another? Right?

Did God really say…? Does that verse really mean…? Are you going to take that literally? What kind of a loving God would _____ (fill in the self-serving blank)?

And that's how stealthily and insidiously the Great Deceiver leads the church astray. He distorts God's Word and presents a new, different gospel to each generation. Eve has caught a lot of flak over the years, but we are no less vulnerable. He can use an apple or a soapbox. Trust us, the Great Deceiver knows the deceitfulness in our hearts (Jeremiah 17:9) and is well acquainted with our carnal desire to rule and worship ourselves. He's happy to show us how.

But we don't have to be duped. Despite the myriad of compelling arguments or the charisma and charm of influencers, we can still discern who is preaching a different gospel. We are called and empowered to detect the one-off renditions of Jesus.

Jesus told the disciples, "Watch out that no one deceives you" (Matthew 24:4 NIV). The warning was regarding His return, but it's applicable to every biblical topic and all aspects of our Christian walk. There's only one way to prevent the Great Deceiver from having great influence in our lives. We are to focus on Jesus Christ, His truth, His words, and the gospel He came to personify, proclaim, and die for so that we would never be separated from God.

PRAYER FOCUS

Spend some time praising God that you don't have to be deceived and that you have access to the real gospel. Ask the Lord to reveal any areas where "your truth" and preferences tend to trump His truth and promises.

MOVING FORWARD

o How has the Great Deceiver exploited your feelings, opinions, and personal preferences?

o What are some of the most common ways you see him distorting God's Word and presenting a new gospel within the church today? How has it affected your faith?

o Read John 10:7–10. Jesus is the Good Shepherd, and we are His sheep. What can you do to ensure you recognize His voice and follow Him alone?

ALL YOUR HEART

"Love the Lord your God with all your heart
and with all your soul and with all your mind."

MATTHEW 22:37 NIV

Statistically speaking, not that many people hated Jesus. As in, hated Him so much that they wanted Him dead. But there were a few. A group from Jesus' hometown tried to push Him off a cliff after He compared them to the wicked citizens of Elijah's day. They failed to kill Him, which, incidentally, means they also failed to prove Him wrong. Likewise, there were the ridiculous Pharisees and teachers of the law. They were relentless in their pursuit of Jesus and obsessed with taking Him down. Some were so rabid with hatred that benefitting from Jesus' death was all they could think about. It governed their every move.

And don't forget the bloodthirsty lunatics who urged Pilate

to crucify Jesus. For sure, they wanted Him dead. Their hatred for Jesus wasn't even personal—they were just feeding their lustful appetites. Pilate's proposition was like throwing chum to a gam of circling sharks.

Needless to say, those were extreme responses. Not everyone was like that; the average villager certainly wasn't. Most of them were not incensed with blind rage, plotting Jesus' murder, or gleefully waiting for it to happen. The average villager was, well, average and likely thinking more about his daily life than somebody else's death. Ergo, you'd think the average villager was better off than the homicidal maniacs.

But then Jesus started talking about love.

When the Pharisees asked Jesus which commandment was the greatest in the law, He replied, "'Love the Lord your God with all your heart and with all your soul and with all your mind.' This is the first and greatest commandment. And the second is like it: 'Love your neighbor as yourself'" (Matthew 22:37–39 NIV).

Jesus' answer encompassed every law. In other words, *if you do these two things, the rest should take care of itself.* That shut the Pharisees up because there was nothing left to debate, but it also leveled the playing field. Suddenly, the average villager lost his advantage over the lunatics—because the opposite of loving Jesus isn't hating Jesus, as the lunatics did. The opposite of loving Jesus is loving yourself more.

This is where we need a heart check. Of course there will always be people who are ardently opposed to Christ.

But there are far more average villagers in the world who are indifferent to what He has to say. And neither works.

Loving the Lord our God with all our hearts actually means that our response to Him must be extreme. It means we must be relentless in our pursuit and obsessed with lifting Him up. If we're not captivated by how we benefit from Jesus' death, we'll never allow Him to govern our every move. We'll stay lustful in our appetites and continually feed on the things of this world. To truly love Him means that being an average villager is no longer an option. Instead we must love ourselves less and hate our sin more—as in, hate it so much we want it dead. We must die to ourselves so that we can love Him more fully.

So that we can love Him with all our hearts.

PRAYER FOCUS

Thank Him for the privilege of being able to love the Lord with all your heart, soul, and mind. Ask Him to help you respond appropriately... to the extreme. Thank Him for being willing and trustworthy to govern your every move.

MOVING FORWARD

o Is your default setting "average villager"? What is something you can do this week to help shift your focus from your daily life to your spiritual life?

o   Are there areas in your life where you tend to feed on things of the world? Money, entertainment, food, social media, etc.? How does this hinder loving the Lord with all of your heart?

o   Are there sins you need to hate more than you do? Ask the Lord to reveal what needs to change in your heart, soul, and mind in order for you to love Him fully.

THE JUST

[Jesus] entered the temple and [with a whip of cords] began to drive out those who sold and those who bought in the temple, and he overturned the tables of the money-changers and the seats of those who sold pigeons. And he would not allow anyone to carry anything through the temple. And he was teaching them and saying to them, "Is it not written, 'My house shall be called a house of prayer for all the nations'? But you have made it a den of robbers."

MARK 11:15–17

The notion that Jesus was "just a good teacher of nice things," as so many people throughout society have concluded, is patently ridiculous. Not only did He claim to be God numerous times (which would make Him a crazy person if it weren't true), but His disciples also continued to proclaim His deity long after He was gone. In fact, most of them were put to death when they refused to *un*claim it. Jesus called religious leaders snakes and vipers (Matthew 12:34), cursed a fig tree for not bearing figs when figs weren't even in season (Mark 11:12–14), and preached that unless "you eat the flesh of the Son of Man and drink his blood, you have no life in you" (John 6:53), all of which actually make sense when studied in context, but none of which sound particularly *nice*.

Neither does fashioning a whip and chasing people with it. But that's exactly what Jesus did when He saw men exploiting the people and capitalizing on worship and prayer inside the temple walls—and it put everyone around Him on notice: Jesus wasn't someone to be trifled with. Up until that moment, the disciples had witnessed other-worldly preaching accompanied by miracles; they and so many others had been drawn in by an indescribable love. But in this moment, Jesus was displaying a very different side, and we can only imagine that His followers were wide-eyed.

Admittedly, when it comes to preaching, the *love* of Jesus makes for a better sell because people are drawn to things that feel good. But the truth is that without the opposing balance of *justice*, love loses its meaning. For instance, it's not loving to overlook a crime. Only a fool would advocate for a system that offers no justice because not only does justice punish bad behavior, but it also acts as a deterrent for future bad behavior, which makes it not only *right* but also necessary, good, and, in the long run, loving.

And while it's true that Jesus came to save us from the consequences of our sin—the punishment we've earned and rightly deserve—He didn't erase our sentence. Instead He took it upon Himself so that our relationship with a just and loving God could be restored. That kind of love *is* beautiful and perfect and worthy of being preached until, like the disciples, we breathe our last breath.

But if we refuse Him, make no mistake—He will be the implementor of justice.

"For we must all appear before the judgment seat of Christ, so that each one may receive what is due for what he has done in the body, whether good or evil" (2 Corinthians 5:10).

Jesus is love. And Jesus is just. He created the world, and He rules over it, and we will be accountable to Him for the choices we make.

We will be accountable for our response to His love.

PRAYER FOCUS

Hebrews 4:16 says God wants us to draw near to His throne with confidence so that we may receive mercy and find grace to help in [our] time of need. But we must also never forget He's King of the universe, holy, just, and intolerant of sin. And so take time today to kneel in prayer as a symbol of your reverence for who He is and what He's done.

MOVING FORWARD

o   Read John 1:1–5 (sidebar: "The Word" = Jesus), Romans 3:23–26, Romans 5:8, and Revelation 22:12–13 and write down *all* the attributes of Jesus that they include.

o   Explain how these character qualities are consistent with Jesus' behavior in the temple.

o How should knowing that God is both just and loving alter the way you think, behave, and move forward in your walk with Him?

COMPASSION

Jesus went through all the towns and villages, teaching in their synagogues, proclaiming the good news of the kingdom and healing every disease and sickness. When he saw the crowds, he had compassion on them, because they were harassed and helpless, like sheep without a shepherd.

MATTHEW 9:35–36 NIV

Jesus taught those who suffer. That's what He came to do.

> Blessed are the poor in spirit,
> for theirs is the kingdom of heaven.

> Blessed are those who mourn,
> for they will be comforted. …

Blessed are those who are persecuted because
of righteousness,
for theirs is the kingdom of heaven. (Matthew
5:3–4, 10 NIV)

Jesus touched those who suffer. That's what He came to do.

A man with leprosy came and knelt before
him and said, "Lord, if you are willing, you can
make me clean." Jesus reached out his hand and
touched the man. "I am willing," he said. "Be
clean!" (Matthew 8:2–3 NIV)

Jesus suffered for those who suffer. That's what He came to do.

He was despised and rejected by mankind, a
man of suffering, and familiar with pain. Like
one from whom people hide their faces he was
despised, and we held him in low esteem. Surely
he took up our pain and bore our suffering, yet
we considered him punished by God, stricken
by him, and afflicted. (Isaiah 53:3–4 NIV)

Jesus invited those who suffer. That's what He came to do.

"Come to me, all you who labor and are heavy
laden, and I will give you rest. Take my yoke
upon you, and learn from me, for I am gentle
and lowly in heart, and you will find rest for your
souls." (Matthew 11:28–29)

Jesus led those who suffer. That's what He came to do.

> The Lord is my shepherd; I shall not want.
> He makes me lie down in green pastures.
> He leads me beside still waters.
> He restores my soul.
> He leads me in the path of righteousness
> For his name's sake. (Psalm 23:1–3)

Jesus has compassion for those who suffer. That's what He continues to do.

Before Jesus hung on a cross. Before He touched the sick and diseased. Before He taught in a synagogue or preached His first message, Jesus expressed His deep compassion for man by becoming one. He was the incarnate expression of His Father's tender heart toward His sheep.

Without Him, we are as harassed and helpless as the crowds Jesus walked through. He knows our needs. He sees our suffering. He understands our pain. It is by His wounds we are healed and through His Spirit we are taught, touched, invited, and led. That is compassion. That is perfect love.

PRAYER FOCUS

Thank the Lord for His limitless compassion and perfect love. Ask Him to reveal more of His truth and character in times of suffering. Praise Him for being your leader.

MOVING FORWARD

o How has Jesus taught, touched, invited, and led you in your suffering?

o Which of these verses most resonates with you and why? Write it on a piece of paper and tape it where you'll see it each day.

o In what ways has Jesus' compassion been most evident in your life or in the lives of those around you?

JESUS IS

It happened that as he was praying alone, the disciples were with him. And he asked them, "Who do the crowds say that I am?" And they answered, "John the Baptist. But others say, Elijah, and others, that one of the prophets of old has risen." Then he said to them, "But who do you say that I am?" And Peter answered, "The Christ of God."

LUKE 9:18–20

It's fitting to end this book the way it began: with Jesus, His followers, and the most important question in the history of humans.

Peter was convinced, and rightly so. He had witnessed Jesus perform miracles and teach with other-worldly authority and wisdom. He'd also spent time with Jesus away from the crowds, experiencing His presence and personhood firsthand and on a daily basis. Which meant Peter had seen Jesus' genuine love for people. He'd seen Jesus pray. He'd seen Him turn the other cheek and rely wholly on the Father for direction and provision. He'd looked into Jesus' eyes and had no doubt seen what many of us can't wait to someday see—the Creator of the universe and lover of our souls looking back. So yeah, contrary to the public speculation, Peter knew that Jesus wasn't like the great men of faith who came before Him—He far surpassed them all.

Who do you say that I am?

It's easy to answer that question correctly when life makes sense—when things are going well and the path seems straight. But it's a whole other thing when life veers into a ditch. Off-roading brings feelings of abandonment. *Where are you God? Why is this happening? How could you allow it?* Ditches are oft the precursor to crises of faith because they don't always align with who we think Jesus is. In other words, when God disappoints, fear and doubt and a host of other emotions set in, calling into question His character and sometimes His very existence.

When Peter was sitting face-to-face with Jesus, everything was so clear. He was sincere in his answers and eager in his commitment to follow. But fast forward to Jesus' death, resurrection, and one of the last moments Peter would spend with Jesus on earth:

> Jesus said to him, …"Truly, truly, I say to you, when you were young, you used to dress yourself and walk wherever you wanted, but when you are old, you will stretch out your hands, and another will dress you and carry you where you do not want to go." (This he said

to show by what kind of death [Peter] was to glorify God.) And after saying this he said to him, "Follow me." (John 21:17–19)

A time was coming for Peter when his faith would make him a martyr, crucified on a cross like his Savior. And while most of us won't face such an extreme testing of our belief, the fundamental question remains:

Who do you say that I am?

In the face of cancer, persecution, abuse, loneliness, a global pandemic, the loss of a job or of someone you love—who is Jesus then? We have found that when life causes our souls to faint and our faith to fail, Scripture does not.

Jesus prays for us.

"Christ Jesus is the one who died—more than that, who was raised—who is at the right hand of God, who indeed is interceding for us" (Romans 8:34).

Jesus forgives us and renews us.

"Repent, then, and turn to God, so that your sins may be wiped out and that times of refreshing may come from the Lord" (Acts 3:19 NIV).

Jesus guides and keeps us.

"My sheep listen to my voice; I know them, and they follow me. I give them eternal life, and they shall never perish; no one will snatch them out of my hand" (John 10:27–28 NIV).

Jesus is the lover of our souls.

"Because of his great love for us, God, who is rich in mercy, made us alive with Christ even when we were dead in transgressions—it is by grace you have been saved" (Ephesians 2:4–5 NIV).

Jesus is the Christ of God.

"For God so loved the world, that he gave his only Son, that whoever believes in him should not perish but have eternal life" (John 3:16).

PRAYER FOCUS

Who do you say Jesus is? Tell Him. And remember, prayers aren't always pretty. God wants us to be honest in prayer so that everything is on the table—and then He meets us there.

MOVING FORWARD

o Peter was an authentic guy. Translation: he wore his messy heart on his sleeve. What messy thing in your life sometimes causes you to question or doubt Jesus?

o Read Revelation 22:1–5. Jesus Christ came to save us from sin so He could take us to heaven. How does reading about heaven alter the way you see your circumstances?

o Make a list of Christ's attributes and then pray them back to Him: *Jesus, you are… You are…You are… You are …*

ABOUT THE AUTHORS

Amanda Jenkins is an author, speaker, and mother of four. She has written five books, including *Confessions of a Raging Perfectionist*, a memoir that has inspired women's Bible studies and conferences all over the country. She specializes in writing and teaching raw authenticity in our faith, which was the intent behind *The Chosen* devotionals. She lives just outside of Chicago with her children and husband, Dallas.

Kristen Hendricks is an author, artist, and the creator of Small Girl Design. Before illustrating (literally) how a Big God can work through a Small Girl, Kristen witnessed this truth time and again during her tenure as executive director of an anti-trafficking organization in East Africa. Kristen lives in the Chicago area with her two daughters and husband, Joe, where she strives to champion for women and point them to Christ.

Dallas Jenkins has been a filmmaker for over twenty years. He is currently producing *The Chosen*, the first multi-season show about the life of Christ. He's produced or directed over a dozen films, including *What If...* and *The Resurrection of Gavin Stone*. The viral success of his short films about the Gospels from a different perspective led to his current series, *The Chosen*, and this devotional. He is also a sought-after speaker, blogger, and media guest on pop culture and faith topics.